Change Your Trajectory is one of the best books I have ever read. Two things that happened as I read…my intellect was stimulated with the new knowledge I gained and my spirit was inspired by the hope you find in Bishop Bronner's pen. It's always a great joy when I can find a book that talks of the next big thing before it is the next big thing. As a leader and innovator I found that the words in *Change Your Trajectory* are words not many have spoken or yet written about. *Change Your Trajectory* does more than just help you maintain success; it also helps you in developing a positive inner drive and steps toward reaching your goals and dreams. If you are a minister, business leader, or even a congressional leader, here is a book that can help you sustain and further your goals and purpose. A great read for corporate America leaders and those who work on the front lines of America.

—*Richard P. Montanez*
Pepsi Marketing and Sales
Inventor of Flaming Hot Cheetos

Transitions are never easy. Unfortunately, they're also inevitable. In *Change Your Trajectory*, Bishop Bronner reveals the secrets to thinking, acting, and responding in a way that turns even the toughest of transitions into a change for the good.

—*Dr. Larry Osborne*
Pastor, North Coast Church
Vista, CA
Author, Accidental Pharisees and Sticky Church

Personal, relational, professional, and cultural seasons of transition can be confusing, disruptive, and painful. *Change Your Trajectory* is the perfect literary GPS tool to navigate you through any moment of transition efficiently and effectively. This book will you get you through your "right now" and to your next destination successfully!

—*Charles Jenkins*
FellowshipChicago.com
Senior pastor & gospel recording artist

I love the optimism and hope that Bishop Dale Bronner brings to all of us facing the challenges of a changing world, a changing landscape, and the ever-changing journey called life. *Change Your Trajectory* brings together the critical tension of knowing that God is always with us in the midst of change and owning that He has given us the power not only to face every change, but to embrace change as an opportunity to create a change that makes us better, our lives better, and the world better!

—*Erwin Raphael McManus*
Founder of Mosaic Los Angeles
Author of The Artisan Soul

In the midst of change, adversity is inevitable. No matter the circumstance or situation, Dale C. Bronner's *Change Your Trajectory* is a powerful and inspirational guide to shifting paths and experiencing God's full blessing in our lives.

—*Steven Furtick*
Lead pastor, Elevation Church
Charlotte, NC
New York Times best-selling author of *Crash the Chatterbox, Greater,*
and *Sun Stand Still*

Change is inevitable, but what you choose to do in the midst of it is up to you. In his new book, my friend Dale C. Bronner encourages you to see the God-opportunities in change. *Change Your Trajectory* gives practical steps to becoming a master of change rather than a victim.

—*John Bevere*
Author and minister
Messenger International

Life is all about change. Every stage we enter requires it, and along with those changes come inevitable conflicts. But that's not the end. In his latest book, *Change Your Trajectory*, Dale C. Bronner shows readers that when we are willing to make the changes God wants us to, we will experience the growth God has for us. It's a cycle of success: change, conflict, growth. This book is a must read for anyone ready to experience that growth!

—*Ed Young*
Pastor, Fellowship Church
Grapevine, TX
New York Times best-selling author of *Sexperiment* and *The Creative Leader*

DALE C. BRONNER

CHANGE YOUR TRAJECTORY

WHITAKER
HOUSE

CHANGE YOUR TRAJECTORY:
Make the Rest of Your Life Better

Dale Bronner
212 Riverside Pkwy
Austell, GA 30168
contact@woffamily.org
www.woffamily.org

ISBN: 978-1-62911-552-8
eBook ISBN: 978-1-62911-574-0
Printed in the United States of America
© 2015 by Dale Bronner

Whitaker House
1030 Hunt Valley Circle
New Kensington, PA 15068
www.whitakerhouse.com

Library of Congress Cataloging-in-Publication Data

Bronner, Dale C., 1962–
  Change your trajectory : make the rest of your life better / Dale Bronner.
    pages cm
  ISBN 978-1-62911-552-8 (trade pbk. : alk. paper) — ISBN 978-1-62911-574-0 (ebook)
  1. Change (Psychology)—Religious aspects—Christianity. I. Title.
  BV4599.5.C44B76 2015
  248.4—dc23
                2015020834

1 2 3 4 5 6 7 8 9 10 11 ⨆ 22 21 20 19 18 17 16 15

Acknowledgments

As John Donne wrote, "No man is an island entire of itself…," so I have to acknowledge a host of people who have influenced my life and changed my trajectory many times. What normally changes a person's trajectory is the influence of another person who serves as a catalyst in your life. Sometimes my trajectory has been changed because of who entered my life; other times it was changed because of who exited my life.

I am eternally grateful for the many mentors who have guided my life and helped me to become who I am today. As I rhapsodize about my incredible journey in life, I want to acknowledge my first heroes, my dad and mom, the late Mr. Nathaniel Bronner and Mrs. Robbie Bronner. They loved me, challenged me, encouraged me, and supported me in an exceptional way! I began my ministry in their home where I taught for thirteen years.

I want to acknowledge my sixth grade teacher, the late Mrs. Sylvia Sewell, who gave me a love for English, grammar, and poetry. I want to thank my high school Spanish teacher, Dr. Shirley Kilgore, for creating a love in me for the Spanish language and for making learning it fun! I am deeply grateful to Dr. Anibal Bueno, my college philosophy professor who challenged me to think deeply about truth. I am profoundly appreciative to Dr. Ronald Cottle, who made Hebrew and Greek come alive for me while I was working on my doctorate.

I was licensed and ordained in the ministry at the tender age of eighteen years old because of the prophetic voice of my pastor, Rev. Dr. William Holmes Borders, Sr. I am thankful he saw the call of God upon my life before I even recognized it. Then he ordained me and prayed the prayer of installation in my first pastorate.

My life hit another huge trajectory when I married the love of my life, my high school sweetheart, Dr. Nina Bronner, who birthed five wonderful children for me. She is my encourager, my confidant, my life partner, and my friend.

I want to acknowledge the late Dr. Edwin Louis Cole for being a true spiritual father in my life and Dr. John C. Maxwell for his personal mentorship. I also want to acknowledge the mentorship of Dr. John Haggai whose wisdom has saved me from some costly mistakes. He is a wealth of encouragement and an uncompromising Bible stalwart.

I want to acknowledge the impact that my friend, Dr. Joel Katz, has had on my life. He has broadened my horizons and given me experiences that set me on new trajectories. I am continually grateful for all the relationships God has brought into my life. Each one has made a unique contribution and impacted me in a positive way.

Finally I wish to acknowledge the wonderful staff and leadership of Whitaker House for believing in me and making the investment to make this book possible.

Ultimately, I acknowledge that all that I am is by the amazing grace of God!

Contents

Foreword

When I was first exposed to the exciting concept that would become the substratum of the book, *Change Your Trajectory*, my mind went back to another time in our history. The year was 1978, the writer was Bernard Ighner, the psalmist was the incomparable Nina Simone; coupled with the legendary production of Mr. Quincy Jones, they collaborated to produce a song that resonated with the times. That song was called "Everything Must Change," and it poured out a truth that has only escalated in its equity and value as times moved forward. "There are not many things in life you can be sure of," it declared. This was true even in 1978, but today it isn't just the certainty of change that's true, but the pace at which the changes come. Faster than the rushing tide of a tsunami, the world wakes up each day to find that none of the absolutes of yesterday are still stable. The pressure and pace of change has made yesterday's solutions obsolete by morning light. It keeps us all on the cutting edge of creativity—or on the edge of a bridge contemplating a leap into the chilling waters of defeat!

While some have succumbed to indifference and others to decline, not one of us can say that we haven't been dismayed with each new headline of Fortune 500 companies selling, marriages terminating, stock markets crashing, and gas prices falling and rising. Our society is changing at breakneck speed, and our world is full to the brim with changing values, fluctuations of property values, and changing trends in retail. Nina belted out the song's lyrics, "There are not many things in life you can be sure of." When all around us began to sink, shift, and shatter, we seek a strategic edge to which we can face the uncertain with a stability that transcends and is not predicated upon external circumstances to sustain itself. Nina was right!

One wonders, is a crystal ball needed to know in whom and for what we can align our efforts in order to provide stable, strategic reliability? We seek to find opportunities to influence and effect culture from an anchored spot that hasn't been engulfed by the current or swept up in the newest wave or changing poll.

We cannot change the world from an eye-level view. We must gain altitude to see exactly what we can do from a proactive perspective. Whether you are leading an army, a ministry, a company, or a household, there is a degree of pressure and stress inherent simply because we dwell in the midst of uncertain times and unstable people and all of us have a desire to succeed in spite of the environment.

The uniqueness of Dr. Dale Bronner's vision could in part be from the rare advantage inherited from the late Mr. Nathaniel Hawthorne Bronner, his father. Bronner Sr. defied the odds and overcame the quagmire of the not-too-distant Depression and the racial unrest of the times. He was a black man who, in 1947, built the multimillion-dollar brand, The Bronner Brothers, an empire of hair care products. The apple didn't fall far from the tree! Dale Bronner was sired in the midst of, raised in the room with, defiant leadership! Consequently, he brings us the wealth of wisdom from all who were before him. He has found a stable place through which you and I can navigate the changes of our times and remain not only productive, but even flourish in a climate that is often as unpredictable as an adjustable rate mortgage!

This deep thinker has his hands full. On one hand, he has the sense of business inherent to the family industry from which he is derived. On the other hand, Dr. Bronner also sits at the helm of the Word of Faith Family Worship Cathedral—a highly respected megachurch model, giving oversight to thousands of deeply intellectual thought leaders, business owners, and family caregivers. So, through the duality of both hands, we receive the gift of faith and finance, the secular and the sacred. He speaks to both needs with comfort and without violating the tenets of either. His commentary can extrapolate trends from the wide array of influences he has at his disposal to ascertain what does and does not work. He reminds us that inflexible people will be devoured by the change while proactive people are dining on the succulent opportunities that are often unnoticed in such climates of change.

His book, *Change Your Trajectory*, is a clear voice speaking through a GPS system on a winding road, providing clear, concise direction and recalibration when necessary for those who have a need to reroute their lives and rebound into a more relevant posture.

The question remains, with all the changes around us, what changes need to be made within us? Our thoughts, our organizational structure, our associations, our staff, all are scrutinized by this literary work that blows the horn in our ears so that we will not succumb to the ever-increasing casualties of change. It would be enough if Bronner's book only hoped to rescue us from calamity, but he has far exceeded that goal by presenting principles that enable some to surf in environments to which others succumb. If you want to ride the waves of change you will definitely have to make some changes. People like myself realize the liquidity of thought and the nimbleness of mind necessary to succeed in this current environment. But what excites me most about this book is how Bronner digs deeply into the specificity of the particulars, showing us *what* needs to be changed and *why* it needs to be changed to transform the adversity into unrealized opportunity.

I've known Dr. Bronner for many years. I've seen him build, buy, lead, parent, and prosper as he engages us all to be better and deeper thinkers. His ambidextrous ability to remain relevant in the faith space, without losing his relevance in the business world, is unrivalled. He has both lectured and ministered around the world. His business acumen brings a much broader discussion to the topic of change that has often been ignored by traditional faith-based material.

The lyrics of "Everything Must Change" later croon, "And mysteries do unfold." This book beckons us to see the unfolding of sheer revelation. Whether by land, air, or sea, you will want to take this journey. All aboard? You are about to lift off the runway of the humdrum, familiar life you live, into a much higher dimension of enthusiastic preparation and thought that will prepare you to finish strong! Get out of the back of the bus, sitting as a victim of a system; we were called to change! Those who lead and succeed differ from those who fail, vacillate, and deteriorate in their accomplishments only by the level in which they think and plan their next moves.

So, I caution you to fasten your seat belts, store your traditionalism under the cabin seat, and prepare to lift off into the galling winds of change with the power you need to maintain upward thrust. I encourage you to take a deep breath and turn the page, into a book that will change your life. Ladies and gentlemen, we are cleared for takeoff! Turn the page and lift the wheels of your mind; it's time to change the game!

—*Bishop T. D. Jakes*
CEO, TDJ Enterprises
New York Times best-selling author

PART ONE:

Facing and Embracing
Today's Uncertainty

1

The New Normal: Change and Uncertainty

So much happens in life that we just don't see coming. When we finally think we've figured life out, it has a way of throwing a monkey wrench into the program, discombobulating our plans. You get married so you'll live happily ever after, but in between the marriage and the happily ever after, issues intrude and your happiness evaporates. You take a new job or start a new career or found a new business, but unforeseen obstacles crowd in, and you soon realize the bottom has fallen out of your dream (and your wallet). You go for a medical examination, and the doctor gives you a report that rocks your foundations. Or you have an accident, and in just one split second you who were so strong and self-dependent are incapacitated—now you need somebody else to serve you hand and foot when you've been so used to serving yourself. Or after one explosive conversation, a friendship or a loving relationship that you thought was solid is now seriously jeopardized.

So quickly, your entire existence as you know it can turn upside down. There's no doubt about it: you will go through personal earthquakes and tsunamis that shake your life, throw you off balance, and leave you asking, "God, how am I supposed to respond to this? How could You let this happen?"

The Range of Change

Such uncertainty has always been a factor on the personal level, but now—more than ever, I think—it's true on the cultural level as well. All around us, everywhere, there's rapid change. Uncertainty is the new normal. We see perpetual changes in technology, in communications, in transportation, in economics, in government, and in politics. Change is rampant in every industry and every trade: in manufacturing, electronics, food processing, marketing, publishing, finance, construction, insurance, health care, education, entertainment—every arena has been dramatically changed. It's true not just in our country, but everywhere; throughout the world we're seeing seismic shifts, upheavals, and transformations.

← UNCERTAINTY IS THE NEW NORMAL. →

Think about the Middle East—how ISIS came out of nowhere and ate up territory in mere months. Look at the division, the lives lost, the priceless, historical treasures that were destroyed in a second. Think about the conflict in Ukraine, or the economic problems ravaging Europe. Think about how many dictators throughout the world have risen, ruled, and then fallen, just in your lifetime! And you're sitting on the couch in front of the TV, saying "I thought that guy would never lose power!"

Imagine that you were born several decades ago, but for most of your life you've been in a coma and just now woke up. Why, you wouldn't even know how to conduct yourself in these times! All this constant change seems to be built right into the system of how our modern world works—if things weren't constantly changing, our world as we know it would collapse. Our culture is in a frenzied pursuit of developing better, and better, and then even better ways of doing things, and it's trickling down to our daily life.

Take electronics, the most visible example. It's totally expected that in a matter of months, or a few years at most, you're going to need a new cell phone, an updated computer plus a constant stream of new software, an enhanced TV setup, and a new and better model of every other electronic device you happen to own. In your grandmother's day, if you told her, "Grandmamma, you're going to need a new phone soon," she would answer, "No, baby, my phone's working fine." As long as she had a dial tone, she certainly was not going to buy a new telephone! But people are no longer expected to think and act that way.

Technology has even changed how you do your grocery shopping. Years ago, if you grew up in a small town (as most of us did) and shopped at its grocery store, you could just go in, get your goods, and tell the clerk to put it on your account. You didn't even need money because everybody knew you! They would just keep track of it at the store, and say, "Miss Wilson, she got $25 worth today." I remember back in the day, my mother would go in the grocery store and get six bags of groceries and it'd come out to $25. Today you get a loaf of bread and a bag of potato chips, and it's $25! Everything has changed.

Ebb and Flow

In this book, I'm going to help you fully grasp the meaning of this simple fact: *Change is occurring.* It is constant change, all-encompassing change, with a variety of effects. It's like the shore of the sea—every time something from the deep washes in, something else is washing back out.

We can often feel that we ourselves are being swept up and carried off by those tidal movements. Sometimes God is bringing you to the forefront, and it's like He's saying, "It's your time! It's your time! It's your time!" In other seasons, aspects of our lives that have been on the forefront are being washed back out, and we can hear the voice sounding, "Time's up! Time's up! Time's up!"

Perhaps you've been frustrated and feeling unable to move forward. You've been sitting back watching others get blessed with new houses, new husbands and new wives, new jobs, new titles, new positions; you've seen them live their dream and do their thing, and you've wondered, *Lord, when will my time come?* You've been watching folks playing the double-dutch game of life, jumping rope and having all the fun, laughing and giggling and carrying on while you stand back and wait. Maybe you even got tired of waiting and tried to jump into the action—only to get tangled in the ropes, because it just wasn't your time.

But I assure you and declare to you that in the ebb and flow of all that God is doing, things are getting ready to change!

And that will mean a new trajectory for us. You can trust God to reposition you at the right place at the right time. Every time that something comes in, something is washing back out. Even if you have been disadvantaged because of something, or sidetracked by something, your time is coming when you will be brought to the forefront. Your song is about to sound forth, even as the songs of others grow silent. Some who are unknown now will be brought into prominence; others who currently are in high standing will soon fade into obscurity. This is God's doing, for *"He puts down one, and exalts another"* (Psalm 75:7). God raises up some even while He suppresses others.

Some things are getting ready to trade places, and not by your brains or your manipulation. Just remember that, as we talk about change. It doesn't have to be bad, and it all happens because of the Lord. There are many more things that are getting ready to change now—but it is always the same God who will be glorified.

God Is in the Midst of Change

Sometimes when we're in a time of change, when we're ebbing out, we think God may have taken a little vacation—gone for a walk, or forgotten to check up on us. Well, let me give you this word of comfort: Even if you don't see it, God is in the midst of change. Look at Jacob waking up after a time of wrestling with the Lord: *"Then Jacob awoke from his sleep and said, 'Surely the LORD is in this place...'"*

Here's the catch: *"'...and I did not know it'"* (Genesis 28:16).

Surely God is in this place, *and I did not know it.* Some of you are in a frightening place in your life right now, and God is in that place with you. It's a difficult place. It's an uncomfortable place. It doesn't look like God, and it doesn't feel like God, but God is in that place with you.

He's in your place of brokenness. He's in your place of sickness. He's in your place of divorce. He's in your place of being laid off of your job. He's in your place of being done wrong. You might wonder, *God, why would You let accidents happen to me? Why would You let me deal with stuff that I don't feel like I can handle by myself?* but God is surely in that place, even if, like Jacob, you didn't know it! You didn't realize that He was guiding your footsteps—that He is still guiding your feet!

If you make your bed in hell, God says, "I'm there." If you take wings and fly to the uttermost parts of the sea, God says, "I'm there." Even when darkness is encamped round about you, even there shall God's right hand lead you and guide you. (See Psalm 139.)

God is saying to you, "I'll never leave you nor forsake you. I'll come in your trouble with you. I'll come in your sickness with you. I'll come in your affliction and your persecution. I'll come in there with you. I'll come in the times when you don't feel like you can handle it. I will come into your loneliness and into your isolation with you. I'll come into your brokenness and your contrition. I'll come in there with you."

You may be in places of bewilderment. You may be in places of frustration. You may be in places of confusion. You may be in places of lack. But don't you dare think that you can go somewhere that God is not. I'm here to tell you that in the same way that this precious man Jacob didn't realize God's presence until he woke up, so some of you have fallen asleep—but you are waking out of your slumber now. God is shaking things to wake you up, and when you wake up, you are going to realize that the hand of the Lord was with you all the while.

You'll think that God is judging you, and you will think that He has rejected you and that God is angry with you, but I've got news for you: He loves you. *He loves you.* You are the apple of His eye, He has so much in store for you, and He alone can give you the power to act!

Responding to Change

So what do we do about all this change? Whether we're in an ebb or in a flow, how do we adjust and respond? How do we make our way through all this incredible shifting and uncertainty?

The first thing I want you to be aware of is that *you can have joy in this journey.* Yes, there will be many challenges and surprises and hardships. But it's going to be an incredible journey. Thank God for that!

Second, in these pages you'll encounter many things that can bless your life and give you wisdom for this journey through change. I want to help you make the rest of your life better.

Now it's true that the *best* part of your life comes only when you *leave* this life. God reserves the best for last. When you work for the Lord as a soldier in the army of the Lord down here on this earth, His retirement package is out of this world! It really is! But I also want you to realize that if you learn right now how to place yourself on a certain trajectory of doing things in a certain way—as the Spirit of God is in the process of shifting all of us in so many areas—then you'll also have the opportunity to experience His blessing in so many realms of life in the remaining time He gives you on this earth.

So let's place ourselves on a new trajectory.

2

Change Versus Transition

Change might be happening all around us, but that doesn't mean we understand it. The weather happens around us all the time too, and do we understand the weather? Hardly! Not even the meteorologists do; how many times have they predicted sunshine for the weekend, but then it rained on your party? I can't teach you how to forecast, but I can help you better understand change. To start, let's differentiate between *transition* and *change*—because they're not the same.

What's the Difference?

Transition is the emotional, relational, financial, and psychological processing of change. I want you to hear this very carefully. Whenever we go through a change in our life, it's the transition that throws us; so many of us fail when we are going through the transition. We mess up in transition; we don't handle it well. We get sick in transition because transition takes us to a lot of new and unexpected plans. It's the real culprit: you really have to prepare yourself for the transition, not the change itself.

Instead, the thing that wipes people out is that they don't have sufficient transitional planning. They aren't ready for the emotional rollercoaster they'll experience in times of change, or the transitions in certain relationships that are required, or the adjustments to their finances, or the time and energy needed to psychologically process the change. We neglect transitional planning simply because we haven't thought ahead to all the different areas that change might impact.

TRANSITION, NOT CHANGE, IS THE REAL CULPRIT.

Why do transitions catch us off guard? Because they're *internal*, invisible, so we can't see them coming. They're the stuff that's happening on the inside. As I encounter change, what's happening inside me? How am I dealing with change emotionally, relationally, financially, psychologically? These are internal things. When you get in transition you will go through new pain. Transition is a terribly uncomfortable place for you to be in your life. You will start hurting and not even understand where; you'll think, *I've never hurt like this before. I've never dealt with these kinds of problems. I've never been at this point in my life before.*

Change, on the other hand, is typically *external*. It might be a move to a new location, a job loss, the death of a loved one, a bankruptcy, a debilitating accident or disease, a change in our marital status or family size—all these are external events and matters of change.

All change, however, requires transition; it requires an internal adjustment that our flesh recoils from. We like consistency. That's why we want to just come back and sit in the same seat that we normally sit in and park in the same parking spot. We throw a fit if somebody takes our pew in church. You see, all change involves loss, and we hate that. It involves the loss of the familiar, the loss of what we're comfortable with.

That's why our government, when they want to change something, usually phase it in through a period of five, ten, fifteen years. They want to make the external line up with the internal, so they don't upset anybody and so that it's palatable to us!

But watch out, because it can happen the other way, too; sometimes the internal lines up with the external even when it shouldn't. Sometimes Christians start internally lining themselves up with the external changes that they see in the culture, slowly, until five, ten, fifteen years later, they're miles off the target of what God wanted. Just a little leaven leavens the whole lump, if you give it enough time! That's why we need our Christian doctrine and our stalwart leaders in the faith, who understand what should never change—what is immoveable. Then we can respond to external changes with the right and good internal transitions.

Transitions at Home

You don't have to look far to find the things that launch you into transition and change. I want to share some examples with you, the ones that hit closest to home because they happen right under your roof.

Getting married is a change that certainly throws you into a period of transition. It requires a major shift in your priorities. It takes an emotional adjustment and a financial adjustment, at the very least. As a single person, you got used to buying what you want whenever you want. But now, as a married person, you're always having to check with somebody. Your life isn't just about *you* any longer. Are you married? Maybe you're still in shock, still trying to recover. You're still thinking, *How did…? What happened to me?*

Or how about the birth of children and their entry into your family's life? For one thing, it costs a lot of money to raise children. For another, it requires a lot of effort! At first, you're always being awakened in the middle of the night, and your sleep patterns are completely upended. And then as they grow up, they present all kinds of unique demands and challenges that require you to transition, and this continues right on into dealing with teenagers—when you wonder sometimes if this child of yours has lost his or her mind. Teenagers are deep in the process of transitioning from being a dependent child to becoming an independent adult, so they experience a tremendous transition—as do their parents.

BLESSED ARE THE FLEXIBLE, FOR THEY SHALL NOT BE BENT OUT OF SHAPE.

Another transition brought about by having children is in how you, the parent, view yourself. You gain a vision of how you're a link to another generation. You recall that a chain is only as strong as its weakest link, so you become more aware of your shortcomings—you realize you may not be everything you need and want to be as a parent and that the consequences will extend far beyond your own life.

Likewise the death of a spouse—unexpected or not—brings major transition. It's a traumatizing event that turns your life upside down for a long while, as you experience the emotional, financial, psychological, and other effects of processing this monumental change. Long after the funeral, when the phone calls from friends have ceased and nobody's paying visits to the house anymore, the transition continues. You're always waking up in the middle of the night because you hear something, and now you're the only one in the house to respond. You're constantly made aware of all the things your spouse used to do but is no longer there to do. A divorce can throw you into a similar transition, but sometimes with extra baggage.

Responding to Change and Transition

Since the new normal in today's world is change and uncertainty, along with all the transitions and stress that result, I want to give you an overall, big picture of what we can do about it—how we can get ready and stay ready. We'll have a lot more to say about all this in the chapters to come, but I want to give you some practical help right away. Here are four essential things to start giving your attention to in the midst of change:

Adapt

First, always be willing to adapt, since conditions change and keep changing. You have to stay fast, stay flexible, and stay nimble. Blessed are the flexible, for they shall not be bent out of shape. In uncertain times, as the waves of change come in, you've got to be able to roll with them and keep your head above water.

← ————————————————————

YOU'LL NEVER BE ABLE TO INCREASE WHAT'S IN YOUR *HAND* UNTIL YOU INCREASE WHAT'S IN YOUR *HEAD*.

————————————————————→

This is especially true, for example, in business, where your competition will always be evolving and growing—you have to always be on the cutting edge. Imagine how foolish it would have been for McDonald's to not start serving salads at their restaurants when people became more health-conscious. It couldn't just be burgers and fries anymore for the folks counting their calories. You can go to McDonald's and get some sliced apples—whoever thought? Frappucinos, lattes, salads; McDonald's sure knew how to adapt to demand. When the demand changes, you have to reevaluate things, reengineer things, and restructure things.

Charles Darwin is supposed to have once said, "Survival goes not necessarily to the most intelligent or the strongest of the species, but to the one that is most adaptable to change." You've got to be willing to change your trajectory if you realize you're not on the right path and you're not getting the right results.

Improve

Second, make it your aim to improve yourself. Always *get* better and *do* better. Let constant improvement be your goal. Life is a constant process of evaluating, adapting, adjusting—and then *improving* yourself on the basis of all that. You'll never be able to increase what's in your hand until you increase what's in your head. You will never live on a level beyond what you have the ability to think. Remember it's not what happens *to* you that matters but what happens *in* you that matters.

Never be satisfied fully with how well you're performing at any level. You can be at the top in your field, but don't ever become satisfied with that, because that's the beginning of your decline. As soon as you get comfortable, you're inviting disaster through your front door. Never settle for mediocrity! More on that later, don't worry.

Observe

Third, keep your eyes open. *Observe.* Why do you need to observe? Because you cannot think beyond your exposure; you cannot plan beyond your level of awareness. If you haven't observed a better way, you have no possible changes to propose or implement. Observe people and talk to them, because you can always learn something new by talking to people. You know what you know, but you don't know what they know. Look and listen and *learn.*

Connect

And finally, don't just talk to people, *connect* with people. You learn things when you talk to other people, so let your connections with others lead to more observation and wisdom on your part. You know what *you* know, but you don't know what *they* know. So link up with them, and observe. As you connect with others, be really good to them. Treat others with respect and courtesy. Value people. Love people.

YOU KNOW WHAT *YOU* KNOW, BUT YOU DON'T KNOW WHAT *THEY* KNOW.

These four things—*adapt, improve, observe, connect*—are fundamental approaches that will allow you to respond appropriately to change and to plan appropriately for transition. They're a solid foundation for you in uncertain times. But to gain even more traction for changing your trajectory, let's get a deeper, sharper picture of our environment.

3

Adventure on the Seascape

A s you think about living the rest of your life in a world saturated and swirling with change, what kind of image comes to mind?

I want to suggest an image for you. We've spoken already about the *journey* of responding to change; however, I want you to think of your journey not as a pilgrim walking across a landscape, but as a captain of a sailing ship navigating through restless, uncharted waters. And I'm going to call those waters our *seascape*.

*Land*scape is on solid land; a *sea*scape is on water, where the surface is unstable and constantly in flux. Now at first, this picture may not be very inviting to you. On this churning, swirling seascape, you just might get seasick!

But I declare to you that your life is most alive when you're outside your comfort zone. That's what our life in the realm of the Spirit is really about. Whenever God is trying to do something big for you, He's going to first make you terribly uncomfortable. And He does that because He wants you to come *alive!* It's when you're sitting in a big easy chair, with a bowl of chips, getting so cozy and sleepy, that God will toss you into a situation where you don't know whether you're going to live or die, sink or swim. He's got your attention now—your full attention! And you're standing at high alert thinking, *Lord? Seriously? Why?*

Because God's not interested in your happiness, He's interested in your development. When everything's hunky-dory in your life, when all is well and good, you're lulled into complacency. You don't even have an appetite for the Word of God. But when you're in trouble, everything is unstable; you've lost sight of land, and you're desperately wondering what to do, which direction to take, and where to find help. That's what real life is like—a seascape that makes you seasick.

What This Means

On this kind of seascape, you quickly realize certain things.

First, you truly grasp that *the environment is always changing.* New waves are always pouring in, poised to rock your boat. If you're in a hotel room, gazing out at the ocean, it looks like the scenery is the same; but if you get out on the beach and watch the actual seascape, the waves come in, crest at the shore, and flow out. It's always different, each time. They are constantly moving, and each time the waves come in, they crest at a different dimension. The sea surface swells and falls with peaks and valleys.

GOD'S NOT INTERESTED IN YOUR HAPPINESS, HE'S INTERESTED IN YOUR DEVELOPMENT.

So don't be overwhelmed—the environment around us is moving. Have you ever noticed that children seem different now from when we grew up? And you're thinking, *What's wrong with these kids? Why are they so picky?* Everything around us has changed and will change, at some point.

Second, *the changes happen faster than you can imagine.* You think it's about time for a letup, a pause, a little tranquility for a moment, but the next wave doesn't allow for that, or the next. They just keep rushing and crashing against you.

Third, *you find yourself in new places.* Driven by the waves, you're going in new directions, headed toward new destinations that you may never have imagined. You wonder, God, *where am I going?*

Finally, you realize that *course corrections will be needed* to reach the destination you truly desire, and you have to be willing to make those corrections. You can imagine what would happen to you if you were just lying flat on your back on a float on the ocean, doing nothing, soaking in the sun. You'd soon be drifting, carried someplace new. Even if you weren't moving, everything around you would be constantly shifting. Now, if you were on land, you'd be ok—you'd stay put just fine. But you're not; we're all on a seascape! If we lie back and relax, we'll be swept away. So you'd better be thinking about where you really want to go. Choose the right destination, and set your sails to reach it.

That's why you need the discernment and the wisdom of God in your life on this new, ever-changing seascape. You'll have to employ discernment to know when to be persistent in the course you've decided on, and when to be willing to change course. I want to help you become a master navigator on this seascape. I especially want to help sensitize your ear to the voice of the Lord and to sharpen your discernment in various areas.

Waking Us Up

When you really think about it, you realize we're in a period of history unlike anything else humanity has ever seen. As I mentioned in chapter 1, the world is experiencing major alterations. Systemic change is unfolding. The foundational principles on which our culture and society were based have been in many ways rejected, and much that is strange and new to us is rising on unfamiliar foundations and values. So how do we, as Christians, remain faithful and committed to the right things during such unstable times when everyone else is embracing unfamiliar principles? How do we stay on course when the world often seems to be losing its mind, and morality is rapidly being redefined? Where is our anchor?

SO MUCH HAS CHANGED—YET GOD HAS NOT.

In the midst of this ocean of change, God is saying, "I want to awaken My people." The church, the people of God, have been in a slumber. So God is using a storm to wake up those who are sleeping. He'll let it get so rough, you'll *have* to come alive.

He sends storm after storm until every manmade thing that we took refuge under becomes unstable. What you expected to be steady and unwavering in your job and career is now in upheaval. What you expected to be stable in your relationships—you met this person, and you thought, *we'll grow old together*—this too is now all troubled and shaky. The security you expected in your finances, so you could relax and not have to work so hard—this also is now in turbulence and turmoil. The world seems dark.

We all go through these shadows—the valley of the shadow of death; death of people, death of hopes, death of dreams. *Shadow* means that there's some stuff up ahead, but the details are fuzzy. Our future is in a shadow, and we can't see the details. The Israelites who lived during the Old Testament lived in the shadow of things to come, to be revealed, in the New Testament. But in God—the Father of lights—there is no variableness nor shadow of turning. He is the sun, the center of the universe; everything turns around Him, but He Himself shines brightly, constantly, unchangeably. He's the same yesterday, today, and forever. God does not, cannot, change.

On the seascape of your life, so *much* has changed—yet God has not changed. God is holding your hand through every bit of the uncertainty of change that's hitting your life right now. This is a new time, with the seascape swirling as never before. And *God is going to anchor you.* Now, more than ever, you must have Him as your anchor; He'll keep you from drifting. He will anchor you with the example of blessed men and women who stood true to their faith in bygone years. He will anchor you with the understanding of the things that are constant, the things that will never change, the immutable doctrines of Christianity, because if you get off-base from your Christian philosophy in the name of being contemporary and relevant, you might find yourself sinking down in falsehood. And He will anchor you with a sense of patience and perseverance.

The stuff that in the past would set you off and break you into pieces—now there will be a godly maturity in you that will cause you to raise your hand and bless the Lord and say, "You know what? I'm not going to worry about it. What I've lost can be replaced. It's all right; it's *all right.*" As James writes, *"My brethren, count it all joy when you fall into various trials, knowing that the testing of your faith produces patience"* (James 1:2–3). In your times of testing, I encourage you to let those lost things from the past go. Instead, be hopeful for the future.

In describing Jesus, the book of Hebrews speaks of *"this hope we have as **an anchor of the soul**"* (Hebrews 6:19). Amid all the uncertainty in our world and in our lives today, we are *not* like those who have no hope. We have a blessed future! The powers and authorities of this world can lock up our bodies, but they have no power to lock up our hope.

The Christian is bound to hope, just as a ship is bound to its anchor, and despite whatever we might see or feel, our hope is based on the Word of God that we receive from our loving Father. I'm so glad that He is alive and well, and that whenever there's a trajectory that needs to be changed in our lives, we can fall on our knees before Him and say, "God, show me the way. Let Your word come to me. Lord, I need a word from you."

Hearing His Voice

We need such a word from the Lord when we don't know whether to stop and wait, to go back where we came from, or to run forward into something new. So we say, "I need a word from You, Lord. I need direction. I need to hear Your voice."

Sometimes God is just trying to say that He wants us to draw closer to Him. That's why He allows confusion in our lives, such confusion that we have no idea what in the world we're supposed to do. God wants us to return to fellowship with Him and to enter into deeper fellowship than we've ever known. He's saying, "I want you to come to Me because I delight in that. I delight in having you come to Me in all your consternation. I know you're angry and frustrated and want to pull your hair out. So return to Me and allow Me to speak to your need."

I recall a recent season when, in the Atlanta area, we were experiencing weird things in our weather patterns. We had snow, everywhere, all over, in amounts like I'd never seen it before. Now, whenever things happen that seem so out of the ordinary, there's always a question in my spirit. So I was sitting before the Lord and I asked Him, "Lord, what do these things mean? What meaneth these things?"

I took my Bible, and I said, "Lord, You always knew these things that would happen to us; You knew this stuff way back yonder. There's nothing new to You." I remembered also that when God performed His mighty acts for the children of Israel, He made these things known to His servant Moses in a special way. Although the children of Israel *saw* what happened, God *explained* what had happened—and *why*—when He talked to Moses on the top of the mountain.

Now there's something within me that doesn't just want to *see* what happens; for me it prompts a question, and I say, "Lord, what's this all about?" So in that winter of exceptionally heavy snow for Atlanta and in many other places, when creation was groaning, I asked Him again, "Lord, what do these things mean?"

I will never forget the word of the Lord that was whispered to me as I looked out my window and saw the snow. I heard God say, "It's not new to Me. I saw it years ago, and I spoke about it."

And I responded, "Talk to me now."

Then I heard His voice more clearly than ever from the thirty-seventh chapter of the book of Job. He spoke two verses to me, verses 6 and 7: *"For He says to the snow, 'Fall on the earth'; likewise to the gentle rain and the heavy rain of His strength. He seals the hand of every man, **that all men may know His work.**"*

YOU MIGHT BE ON A SEASCAPE, BUT IT'S JUST A MATTER OF SETTING YOUR SAILS.

When it says there that God *"seals the hand of every man,"* it means that He stops each man in his work. So for folks who are workaholics, who were used to going to work under any and every circumstance, God was saying, "I'll make it where they won't even be able to get in. I'm going to seal the hand of man. I'm going to institute a time of divine Sabbath where My people will slow down and stop. They will be still and know that I am God." And that's what the snow accomplished. All that God had to do was simply say to the snow, *"Fall on the earth."*

God does this *"that all men may know His work."* God has a purpose in everything that He does. Don't ever think that it's just by happenstance. It's by design that comes from an incredible, powerful God.

Carried by the Wind of God

I hope you can sense what God is doing—what He's doing in your family, your church, your community, and throughout the world. All this change, it is all for a glorious reason! There is coming such an open door for the gospel of Jesus Christ around the world! In the places that have been closed, God is pulling down walls again. More walls are going to fall. New frontiers are going to be experienced by His people, by you and me.

God is getting ready to expand our territory. He's doing this for *you*—He's getting you ready to go farther than you've ever gone before, and to keep going all the days of your life. Things that you didn't think you could do and would ever do—well, get ready! You might be on a seascape, but it's just a matter of setting your sails.

And when you set your sails, the wind of God will carry you. You don't have to force your way, even as you battle against the strong currents in the waters. If you try to stand against them by yourself, they have the power to knock you down to your knees. But God will move and propel you into the places He divinely intends for you to be, places you've never been. And the spiritual scenery awaiting you is out of this world!

4

A Time for Everything

Listen, *your time is coming.* I declare to you prophetically that God is getting everything ready. Every crooked place is getting ready to be made straight. Yes, the glory of God is going to be revealed. He's going to equalize some things. He's going to bring balance. There's going to be a shift of power, a divine shifting, and it's already preparing to happen. God is in control. You may have looked at your life and then looked around you, and wondered, *God, when are You going to balance these things out?* He will, because He has given a time for everything.

The wisest man who ever lived, Solomon, penned this famous passage:

> *To everything there is a season, a time for every purpose under heaven: A time to be born, and a time to die; a time to plant, and a time to pluck what is planted; a time to kill, and a time to heal; a time to break down, and a time to build up; a time to weep, and a time to laugh; a time to mourn, and a time to dance; a time to cast away stones, and a time to gather stones; a time to embrace, and a time to refrain from embracing; a time to gain, and a time to lose; a time to keep, and a time to throw away; a time to tear, and a time to sew; a time to keep silence, and a time to speak; a time to love, and a time to hate; a time of war, and a time of peace.*
>
> (Ecclesiastes 3:1–8)

Do you see how many "times" there are? This should be profoundly encouraging to you. The fact that change is always happening, that times are always a-changin', means that your time will come, inevitably and invincibly. Right now is the *time* for you to do four things.

A Time to Trust Him

Like I said at the beginning, some things are getting ready to exchange places. The last shall be made first, and the first last. This will not be by any manipulation of the flesh. You won't have to do anything sneaky or strange in order to get promoted by God. *"When a man's ways please the* Lord, *He makes even his enemies to be at peace with him"* (Proverbs 16:7).

YOUR TIME WILL COME, INEVITABLY AND INVINCIBLY.

I want to let you know that God has brought you into His kingdom for such a time as this.

Lift your hands and say, "Lord, I thank You that this is my time." Tell Him now, "My times are in Your hands! God, do with me what You need to do. What needs to be pulled down in me, pull it down! What needs to be raised up in me, raise it up! Transform what needs to be transformed. Shift me in my thinking, God; shift me in my emotions; shift me in my finances; shift me in my relationships; shift me in my mindset. Shift me! Shift my family, my sons and my daughters, into the place You have prepared for them. O God, as things change around us, may You secure us by the anchor of Your Word, by the anchor of Your blood, by the anchor, Lord Jesus, that never changes in our lives. And we will give You the glory, and the honor, and the praise, forever and ever! In Jesus' name, amen!"

We've seen such uncertainty in everything on this seascape where God has placed us, but there *must* be that degree of uncertainty in order to prove our trust in God. So trust Him! Because He knows exactly where you'll wind up. He's not in any doubt about it. He is confident and sure of your destiny. That's why He says to us, "*I know the plans I have for you.*" God doesn't just *think* these things; He doesn't just *hope* they'll work out for you. No, He tells us, "*For I know the plans I have for you…plans for welfare and not for evil, to give you a future and a hope*" (Jeremiah 29:11 ESV).

GOD HAS A PLAN FOR YOU; GRACE ENABLES YOU TO REACH UP AND GRAB IT.

Let me emphasize again, the Lord's design is *for* you! He's not against you. God is *for* you; God is *with* you; God is *in* you. He knows the plans He has for you, and they're plans to prosper you and not to harm you; they're plans to give you a hope and a future, and to lift you up. God wants to give you better things than you even want for yourself. He wants to make your life better than you've ever had it, all the days of your life. Your latter days ought to be fuller and sweeter than your earlier days, to let you finish this life in peace and fulfillment in the strength and blessing of the Lord. So this is the time to trust Him!

A Time to be Used by Grace

Grace is the divine, enabling ability from God for us to *be* what He has called us to be and to *do* what He has called us to do. That's the grace we're to operate in. God has a plan for you; grace enables you to reach up and grab it. Sometimes people will look at you and at everything going on in your life, and they won't be able to figure out how you can have the time, energy, and resources to be able to sustain all that. But it's no secret; it's all God's grace!

When you have God's grace pouring into your life, your life will become so blessed that stress will begin to disappear, and you'll realize, *This is not my own doing.* Paul said, *"By the grace of God I am what I am"* (1 Corinthians 15:10). He knew that it was all God's grace upon him. The same is true for us; if we're able to do something and do it well, it's because God has *graced* us to do it. So tap into that grace!

As Paul wrote to Timothy, **"Be strong in the grace** *that is in Christ Jesus"* (2 Timothy 2:1). Be strong in that grace, because it is *also in you.* Be strong in that same grace that says, *"I can do all things through Christ who strengthens me"* (Philippians 4:13). That doesn't mean I can just go out and do anything I want to do; no, it means I can do *everything God has ordered and designed for me to do*—all things that pertain to my divine destiny. Through Christ I am graced to do all that I was ordained to do, designed to do, destined to do.

God's grace is in you—and it brings a divine ability that will cause you to rise up in the midst of obstacles and setbacks, in spite of all that. God says, "I knew everything about you before you were born. I knew your weaknesses. I knew your imperfections. I knew your inconsistencies—and I chose anyway to redeem you and to use you, because of My grace."

And when you find this grace in the sight of God—*something happens.*

With all of our issues, all our drama, all our fluctuating back and forth, and all our inconsistencies, God still says, "I'm going to use you. I'm going to still use you—for My glory!"

God's grace means that He will never call you to be something or to do something without His help. It's as if God is saying, "I'm going to write a huge stage play, and I'm going to star you in it, but I will always be the power behind you, giving you a story that's worth telling." It's because of *God* that you have a story to tell—because if there's no deliverance or healing or breakthrough in your story, your story is just depressing, and He is the only One who can bring that deliverance, healing, and breakthrough.

It's when God takes somebody who was homeless, and then, as an act of His own grace, He sovereignly opens doors and allows that person to meet someone who gives them a chance—then you know it was *God*, and the story is exciting! It's when you apply for a job that you are not qualified for and have no hope of getting, yet somebody is willing to take a chance and hire you—all because God was at work setting forth your story. It's when you're able to take care of your children even when you're struggling to pay the bills and have no idea how to make ends meet. *God* will make a way. He'll make a way for *you*.

For some, He'll make a way to be supernaturally sustained by God, so that you can't explain how you're able to take care of all that you've taken care of, or how you've kept food on the table. You can't explain how you've come this far doing as well as you have for this long. You just don't understand how things have fallen into place right at the last minute. You can't comprehend it all, but God says, "I will make a way."

DON'T CLOSE THE BOOK WHEN GOD IS TURNING THE PAGE TO ANOTHER CHAPTER.

It's the element of *God* that makes your story worth telling. You have not reached the glory part of your story yet, so don't close the book when God is turning the page to another chapter. He's not finished! All is well in the end—and if all is not well, it's not the end.

A Time for Obedience

But if we're going to be the star of God's stage play, we need to listen to the director. God is *God*, don't forget, and He's looking for a people who will obey. I'm here to tell you that there's no suitable substitute for obedience. God is calling for obedience from His people, and it's far better than sacrifice. (See Samuel 15:22.) In other words, when we make a big show of our devotion, He's not impressed. But when we follow His laws, it pleases Him deeply. He knows that this obedience is the indication that we really understand His grace, and that we really live in the fullness of His grace.

YOU'RE GETTING READY TO MAKE THE *REST* OF YOUR LIFE THE *BEST* OF YOUR LIFE.

He knows that this obedience by the grace of God will bring us joy. When God in His grace tells you to do something, yet you fail to do it, you're going to lose some of your joy and your happiness. Your peace will be disturbed if you're outside the will of God. That's just one more mark of His grace, because He uses that disturbance of our soul to pull us back into closer fellowship with Him. There are times that I am absolutely convinced that God is backing us into a corner where we don't have any other choice but to stop squirming, to be still, and to hear Him say, "I'm God. I'm in control. You don't rule this." God puts us in our place now and then!

A Time to Celebrate

If you've ever questioned whether God is good, if you've ever let yourself be unimpressed by His grace, if you've ever brushed off disobedience as a "no-biggie," then let your mind run back over some of the stuff you've done that He has forgiven you for—and how He has washed you and cleansed you in the blood of Jesus. You'll really begin to celebrate God in such an incredible way when you remember how God has been so good and gracious to you. Thank Him that He didn't give you what you actually deserved!

And that message of His goodness ought to be *seen* by others in our lives. The essence of His message is that God is good and full of grace, and He is faithful even during the times of trial and temptation in our life. I've been at the bedside of many dying saints, and you can't imagine how inspiring it is for me to hear them blessing God! Neither cancer nor anything else has the power to rob that spirit of joy inside of them. They have found God's grace, and they're beginning already the celebration that they will enjoy for eternity.

When you're in God's will, you can survive hell and high water, tossed and driven by waves crashing and dashing against your life because you've got an Anchor, and you're rooted and grounded in Him. It's a great adventure. Come on and walk on the water with Jesus! You're getting ready to enter the greatest part of your life. You're getting ready to make the *rest* of your life the *best* of your life. Your trajectory is about to change. Hallelujah to the Lamb of God! It's going to be an incredible journey with Him—with never a dull moment, I can promise you that!

5

Telltale Signs of
Your New Trajectory

Some of you might know that you're headed toward a new trajectory. Others might be thinking, *How do I know? What are the signs?* For a little help, let's look at the famous prophet, Elijah the Tishbite. Elijah's life was marked by change, challenges, and uncertainty. As Scripture first introduces us to this prophet in 1 Kings 17, we find him plunged immediately into one of these times of transition.

The familiar story begins like this:

And Elijah the Tishbite, of the inhabitants of Gilead, said to Ahab, "As the LORD God of Israel lives, before whom I stand, there shall not be dew nor rain these years, except at my word." Then the word of the LORD came to him, saying, "Get away from here and turn eastward, and hide by the Brook Cherith, which flows into the Jordan. And it will be that you shall drink from the brook, and I have commanded the ravens to feed you there." So he went and did according to the word of the LORD, for he went and stayed by the Brook Cherith, which flows into the Jordan. The ravens brought him bread and meat in the morning, and bread and meat in the evening; and he drank from the brook. And it happened after a while that the brook dried up, because there had been no rain in the land. (1 Kings 17:1–7)

At great risk to himself, the prophet Elijah had gone before the wicked King Ahab to announce—under the inspiration of the Spirit of God—that Ahab's kingdom would experience a severe drought until that time when Elijah himself proclaimed an end to it. After this announcement, which, as you may have guessed, made Elijah extremely unpopular, the Lord directed Elijah out into the wilderness to a stream of water that eventually dried up. At that point Elijah needed to find a proceeding word of the Lord, giving him direction as to where he should go next and what he should do. He had to change his trajectory.

GOD'S ANSWER TO EVERY PROBLEM IS ALWAYS A PERSON.

Have you ever been in the middle of something that was going well but suddenly dried up? You thought you moved to an area with lots of opportunity, but then you lost your job and can't find a new one. You thought your new church had so much life, but then the pastor leaves and everyone starts drifting apart. You thought your new boyfriend was all that, but suddenly you don't have much to talk about and you're not enjoying his company anymore. Whenever something that used to be flourishing dries up, it means you've got to go in another direction. So look for a proceeding word from God.

That word from the Lord did indeed come to Elijah, as we see in verse 8 of this chapter. This experience, and his further experiences in 1 Kings 17, show us the nine telltale signs that your trajectory is changing.

New People

First of all, when you're on a new trajectory, you will meet new people. Why? Because God's answer to every problem is always a person. Now consequently, the problem is generally always a person as well.

The problem is the wrong person in the wrong place at the wrong time doing the wrong thing. God's answer is the right person in the right place at the right time doing the right thing. When you go through major shifts in your life, God will bring at least one new person into your life—and sometimes several new people.

People Precipitate Change

In verse 8 of Elijah's story in 1 Kings 17, when he's there by the Brook Cherith that had dried up, he hears from the Lord: *"Then the word of the LORD came to him, saying, 'Arise, go to Zarephath, which belongs to Sidon, and dwell there. See, I have commanded a widow there to provide for you'"* (1 Kings 17:8–9).

This widow that God mentions is someone Elijah didn't previously know, but God was directing him to her. God was in the process of introducing her into his life. God was saying, "I've already orchestrated for a widow woman to provide for you there."

On every level of life, we need others to introduce us into new relationships and opportunities and connections. Other people give us entrance to different arenas of the world, at different levels. It's often true that when you reach a certain level and can't get any higher, it's because the folks who are on that level won't let you in; the folks with all the money want to keep all that money. He who has the gold makes the rules. God, if He's going to really change us, will bring in people who know what we don't know. If they knew only what you knew, they wouldn't be on a higher level! You need new relationships to know new things. I'm talking about new levels in every sphere: in your spiritual life, in your family life, in your business life, in your career. In all these spheres, you need others who are beyond your current area of experience, people who are on a higher level.

You may be fearful of this new territory you're entering, but God has people planted along your way to guide you in your new trajectory. You might even hear them say, "Can I help you? Are you looking for something? You look like you're lost," and they'll start filling you in.

God knows that He's put answers in people, so you've got to connect with those folks in order to receive their answers. They have perspectives you don't have. They also hold the keys to other relationships that you need. Sometimes an acquaintance will lead you to someone who will become extremely important in your life. They know that person; they have access to that person, or they know how to gain that access. You'll often be surprised by how this works.

Relationships Influence Us

So don't discount any of the "little" people God brings your way. They might be the greatest gift of God to link you to your healing, to your deliverance, and to your growth and development. You never know. God has His angels planted here and there, disguised as janitors, as maids, as cooks, as hairdressers, as service station attendants, as the bagging guy at the grocery store. Don't ever downplay the people that God places along your path.

THE MAN IS MORE IMPORTANT THAN HIS MESSAGE.

Let me prove this to you. I want you to just think with me for a moment about three sermons over the course of your life that have really impacted you. What three sermons have you heard that changed your life? Now I want to ask you this. Who are three people who have changed your life? Think about three people who came into where you were impacted your life in an incredible way.

Now I bet you anything that it was easier for you to think of three people who have impacted your life than to think of three sermons that have impacted your life. Why? Because people impact us far more than sermons: The man is more important than his message. If you don't believe the man, you won't receive his message. There are people whose message is totally disqualified because of their despicable character.

People impact us and have an incredible effect on us. I can usually trace every success and every failure back to relationship. If you'll just let your mind run back, you can start thinking about a person that messed you up, that jacked your finances up. You were okay until you met...fill in the blank! You know who they are, and you wish you'd never met them! But, on the flip side, your life has been incredibly blessed, impacted, charged, changed, and challenged by people who came in and made you better. You can thank God for the times when He brought a person into your life who stretched you and made you better than what you were before. So we have to learn to be able to embrace people who have the ability to challenge us and stir up the stuff that God put inside us.

The reason that these relationships shake us up and send us on a new trajectory is because those people are truth—and truth always has a changing effect when it slices into our lie-filled world. Jesus said, *"I am the way, the truth, and the life"* (John 4:16). Truth is not merely something that you *say*; truth is a *person*. Are you in relationship with a person of truth in your own life? The Law of the Inner Circle, courtesy of John Maxwell, says, "Those who are closest to you determine your level of success." In other words, you show me your friends, and I'll show you your future.

SHOW ME YOUR FRIENDS, AND I'LL SHOW YOU YOUR FUTURE.

New Problems

Elijah's experience in 1 Kings 17 occurred during a time of drought and famine. At first, when he was by the Brook Cherith, God sent ravens who brought Elijah bread and meat every morning and evening, two meals a day. But then God told him to arise and go to Zarephath, and Elijah didn't have his personal catering company anymore. Instead, God told Elijah, "I have commanded a widow there to provide for you."

But it sure didn't look like provision, once Elijah got to Zarephath. He found the widow that God was leading him to, and, probably weak with hunger from his journey, asked her for food. This was her devastating response: *"As the* LORD *your God lives, I do not have bread, only a handful of flour in a bin, and a little oil in a jar; and see, I am gathering a couple of sticks that I may go in and prepare it for myself and my son, that we may eat it, and die"* (1 Kings 17:12).

Well, that sounds promising, doesn't it? Elijah had found a new person, but she didn't have enough to provide for herself and her son, let alone for Elijah too.

In a new trajectory, in every new stage of life you come to, you'll also experience new problems and pains. You can definitely expect them to show up. You thought you were following the Lord's voice, and He led you right smack-dab into new problems. But this is just the way the world turns; with all growth, problems come. If you're expecting growth in your future, realize that all growth must be financed, and finances can be difficult to obtain. Every time our business grew, we had to get a loan to buy a new building. Growth is costly. To move into a bigger place will cost you more money. When your family grows, it costs you money.

WHY WOULD GOD CONFINE US TO ONE LITTLE CORNER?

Say you just got a new job, and you're so thankful to leave behind your old job because, *man*, there were some issues there, but when you get to your new job, the new people just go and cause new problems! That's just the way the world turns: wherever there are people, there are problems. So in every stage of life, you'll find new challenges and difficulties.

New Places

The third telltale sign of a changing trajectory is a new place—God taking us to where we've never been before.

Elijah went first to a place of refuge alongside the Brook Cherith in the lonely wilderness, but then God sent him far away to the city of Zarephath, a town near the city of Sidon along the Mediterranean seacoast, which was a foreign place to him and outside the borders of his homeland. God put him on the go!

The shifts and changes of life will bring us to new locations. God's guidance so often puts us into motion; it's a moving thing. You may have been to a lot of places already, but listen, you'd better get ready and pack your bags! Because He'll put you on the go, too. Why would God confine us to one little corner? Why would He limit your travels to your own neighborhood? *"The earth is the LORD's, and the fulness thereof!"* (Psalm 24:1).

Most of us no longer live very close to the place where we were born. Think about that; God has brought us to new places already, hasn't He? Well, that's the tip of the iceberg; God's not finished with you yet. He's going to take you places—if not to new physical places, then to new spiritual places.

New Possibilities

You'll find that as God closes one door and then opens another, brand new possibilities are just inside that new room. Change always brings into your life new situations and scenarios that are in the realm of *what can be.*

If you get laid off your job, start thinking about entrepreneurial endeavors that would allow you to work for yourself. Maybe you ought to rethink some things and come out of your comfort zone. You'll find new possibilities on every level—a new possibility residing within every problem.

Remember that God told Elijah, "I have *commanded* this woman to take care of you." But she had a problem; she had only enough oil and flour to make one little cake. She was about to make that cake so she and her child could have one last meal before they died. She was destitute. Here was a significant problem, but it was also a *possibility*. Nothing is impossible with God! So God took that thing that was a problem of life and death and showed them a possibility.

Elijah, responding to the guiding of the Spirit of the Lord, pointed the woman in the direction of the Lord:

> *And Elijah said to her, "Do not fear; go and do as you have said, but make me a small cake from it first, and bring it to me; and afterward make some for yourself and your son. For thus says the LORD God of Israel: 'The bin of flour shall not be used up, nor shall the jar of oil run dry, until the day the LORD sends rain on the earth.'"*　　　　　　　　　　(1 Kings 17:13–14)

By her obedience to Elijah's instructions, the woman honored the Lord—and she was enabled to see God's work on their behalf:

> *So she went away and did according to the word of Elijah; and she and he and her household ate for many days. The bin of flour was not used up, nor did the jar of oil run dry, according to the word of the LORD.*　　　　　　　　　　(1 Kings 17:15–16)

In our new environments, God will make us aware of new possibilities that allow us to honor and obey Him, and receive more of His blessing.

New Perspectives

The new place you're in, the new people you're with, may bring you huge changes of perspective. And these new perspectives are so important. Read what happened next in Elijah's story:

Some time later the son of the woman who owned the house became ill. He grew worse and worse, and finally stopped breathing. She said to Elijah, "What do you have against me, man of God? Did you come to remind me of my sin and kill my son?" "Give me your son," Elijah replied. He took him from her arms, carried him to the upper room where he was staying, and laid him on his bed. Then he cried out to the LORD, "LORD my God, have you brought tragedy even on this widow I am staying with, by causing her son to die?" Then he stretched himself out on the boy three times and cried out to the LORD, "LORD my God, let this boy's life return to him!" The LORD heard Elijah's cry, and the boy's life returned to him, and he lived. Elijah picked up the child and carried him down from the room into the house. He gave him to his mother and said, "Look, your son is alive!" Then the woman said to Elijah, "Now I know that you are a man of God and that the word of the LORD from your mouth is the truth." (1 Kings 17:17–24)

The drama in this account is palpable. Remember that we don't know much about Elijah at this point; this is before his big showdown with the prophets of Baal on Mount Carmel. It's possible that Elijah didn't know much about himself at this time, either! The Bible doesn't say, but this is probably one of the first major miracles that Elijah performed. Perhaps he had no idea of his own power, no idea of how mightily God would be using him. When the widow spoke the incredible words, *"the word of the LORD from your mouth is the truth,"* she was confessing Elijah's identity as a prophet. That was a new perspective of himself that he probably needed to hear from the mouth of another, not himself.

Your outlook determines your outcome, and if you don't get a new perspective, you'll act with the old perspective—which will likely cause errors in judgment. If Elijah didn't have his new perspective of himself as a prophet, he may have totally underestimated himself later. To operate on a new level in life, you need a new perspective.

All change, and every new stage in life, will bring us to a new perspective. That's easy to see in children; when you're ten years old, you aren't the same person you were when you were three. A ten-year-old doesn't think the way a toddler thinks. And a seventeen-year-old doesn't think the same way a ten-year-old thinks. They gain new perspectives because they've grown to another level.

YOUR *OUTLOOK* DETERMINES YOUR *OUTCOME*.

Those new perspectives continue into adulthood, as we reach thirty, forty, or fifty. Our values evolve. And the changes keep coming—whether it's in your tender teens, your teachable twenties, your tireless thirties, your forcible forties, your fearful fifties, your seasoned sixties, your settled seventies, your aching eighties, your nebulous nineties, or your audacious hundreds! Every age will bring you to a different perspective.

Which leads also to this point: when God prophesies to you, He's generally not talking about the context of where you are now; He's speaking about where you're *going*. So be really sensitive to the Spirit of God; realize that not only will you meet new people in new places, and experience new problems and pains, but through all of this God will advance your thinking and develop a new perspective. You'll see life differently.

It's like a relationship you may have had in the past with someone who broke your heart, disappointed you, and made you cry. But later you wonder, *Why did I ever fall for that person?* Here was someone who meant the whole world to you, but now you could easily tell that person, "Joker, you don't have it; I've cried my last tear over you!" The reason you can say that is that your perspective has changed. You're not looking at the world and the people in the world with the same eyes you had before. You've matured through the things you've experienced and the things you've suffered.

New Preparation

The times of great change will also lead you into new preparation. Every level of life will require a new kind of readiness. The higher the level you enter, the greater the preparation needed.

When a civilian goes into military life, the first thing they do is put that civilian through boot camp for intense preparation. We often face a kind of boot camp in the new situations God leads us into. That's what it will take.

Elijah was going through a boot camp for prophets, as it were, when he was in the desert, entirely reliant upon the Lord. He was preparing for when he would need to look to the Lord, not just for daily food, but for a fire to come down from heaven and light up a water-drenched altar. (See 1 Kings 18.)

The will to win without the will to prepare means absolutely nothing. If you want to win in life, but you don't have the will to prepare, you're just fooling yourself. And the kind of preparation you need, as well as the level of preparation required, will change with each new situation. You can't just step forward and say, "Okay, I'm ready." No, you've got to be prepared. The Lord calls us to prepare for what's coming, not just in your lifetime, but also to prepare for the next cosmic event: the return of our Lord. He tells us to keep our lamps full of oil, to always be on the watch, to be ready. (See Matthew 25.)

New Priorities

Life's changes will also give us new priorities. Your priorities will have to be reordered. We see it, for example, in the way we treat our bodies. At first we spend our health trying to gain our wealth; then we spend our wealth trying to regain our health!

Your priorities are reflected in the things that you actually get done. When you're around people who are well into their senior years, they're not talking about chasing dollars. They're talking about making it to their yoga class this afternoon, or getting out for a walk yesterday, or drinking all their juice this morning. They're just trying to survive and keep everything working! They've developed new priorities.

You get old enough, and money is not the primary thing anymore; you just want to feel good. When you get old enough, you're not even concerned about being around smart people; you want to be around *kind* people, around folks who know how to respect and appreciate you and be considerate. Kindness is what really matters. Some of those smart people eventually get bent out of shape and bitter over life. So you prefer kind people.

At every new level of life, your priorities change. When you're raising your children, they're your priority, but then when they're all grown up and gone, that's no longer true. And *you* are certainly not their priority! Of course you will always love your children, and think about them, and pray for them. But in a new season of life, priorities change.

AT FIRST WE SPEND OUR HEALTH TRYING TO GAIN OUR WEALTH; THEN WE SPEND OUR WEALTH TRYING TO REGAIN OUR HEALTH!

New Passions

Here's something else remarkable: life's changes and transitions will bring new passions. When you go from one level to another, things that you used to be crazy over are just not that exciting any more. It's because you've reached a new level.

Let me tell you about Elijah's successor, Elisha, who went on to be a great prophet of the Lord. The Lord told Elijah to anoint Elisha as a prophet. It doesn't say that Elisha knew he was coming, or that he had any idea that his life was about to change dramatically. This is all it says:

So Elijah went from there and found Elisha son of Shaphat. He was plowing with twelve yoke of oxen, and he himself was driving the twelfth pair. Elijah went up to him and threw his cloak around him. Elisha then left his oxen and ran after Elijah. "Let me kiss my father and mother goodbye," he said, "and then I will come with you." (1 Kings 19:19–20)

He didn't even hesitate. He said goodbye to his parents, and then he followed Elijah. He embraced his new calling, his new passion.

There are some passions that you'll grow into; slowly you'll begin to develop a love for different things that didn't matter much when you were younger. Other passions will overwhelm you suddenly and beautifully, like a call from the Lord through the mouth of a prophet. It's amazing how life brings and introduces us to new passions as we mature. Sometimes when you lose somebody special in your life, you feel as though you'll never love again, but you can; if you live long enough, you can. You'll discover new passions.

THERE ARE ONLY TWO KINDS OF PEOPLE IN THE WORLD TO ME: PEOPLE WHO *KNOW* JESUS AND PEOPLE WHO *NEED* TO KNOW HIM!

You ought to be passionate about whatever it is God has given your hand to do and has assigned into your care and responsibility. Because if you don't have passion for it, you're not going to do it well. And if it's *your* assignment from God, nobody else will sense the same passion for it. It's up to you. You've got to show folks and prove to them that you're in love with whatever it is you're doing. Don't think you can take it or leave it; be *engaged* with it. Come to the right realization: "This is it! I've got the stuff!" You've got to be passionate about it.

I've been passionate about Jesus ever since I found Him. When I found Jesus, I found all the peace I have ever needed, and I discovered truth. So I don't just tell people that this is *a way*, a nice alternative to other ways they might consider. No, Jesus is the Savior of the whole world! Everybody ought to know Him! There are only two kinds of people in the world to me: people who *know* Jesus and people who *need* to know Him! I'm passionate about Jesus, Jesus, *Jesus!*

New Provision

Elijah experienced *new provision* from the Lord when he was waiting in the desert and the ravens brought him food each day. The woman and her household in Zarephath experienced *new provision* from the Lord's hand. We, too, will discover new provision as we follow a new trajectory. When you're moving in the right direction you'll end up having greater provision, and you'll live on a higher level than you ever have before.

This is good news! God is not trying to take provision from you; He's trying to give *more* to you. It blesses a parent to see their children do well, and we are the children of God under our Father's care. He will ensure that His children have sufficient supplies and provisions for the new chapters of their lives.

God has seen our need before we even had the need—and He has made provision for it. New provisions are waiting for you when you change your trajectory!

PART TWO:

It's All about You

6

Become a Master,
Not a Victim, of Change

As you respond to all the new things that a new trajectory brings, remember that it's all about you. It's all about you—and I don't mean that it's all focused on you. On the contrary, if your life is focused on you, you're going to be miserable! If you're not focused outside of yourself, you'll be the most miserable, unfulfilled person in the world. Rather, what I mean by that phrase is that the responsibility of responding to change rests with you. You have to be a master, not a victim, of change. I'm sure you've heard teenagers say, when they have missed a family dinner or forgot their homework, "Life happens," or "Life just happened, sorry!" Well, that's not a good enough excuse in real life; you can't just lie around, letting life happen to you. You have to make *things* happen to *life*.

Instead of letting the water come in and drown you, make your intention to build a raft and stay on it, and then use all this raging water around you as something to float your boat! The very thing you can so easily fear, and the thing that could so quickly overwhelm you, is instead what you can use to carry and propel you to your intended destination.

So you ask yourself, *how do I strategically manage this change so I don't become a victim of it?*

Be Aware

Awareness is the beginning of mastering change. Are you attentive and sensitive to the fact *change is happening?* We've talked about the incredibly steep rates of change all around us, in all areas of life. That's because I wanted to shake you up a bit and remind you of what you've already observed but maybe tucked away in your subconscious because you didn't want to deal with it.

It's amazing that when a tsunami is coming, many animals have an instinct telling them to get to higher ground. They have an inner awareness that lets them know something is coming. Now do you think God cares more about animals than He does about us? Of course not. So there ought to be an awareness inside us that's letting us know, "Listen, huge changes are coming; be prepared for them." And as you grow in this awareness—and when you see the telltale signs that something's coming—take enough time to pause, slow down, and really think about your situation. You need a clear, focused mind when dealing with change.

As you slow down like that, take a deep breath. Our stress-induced tendency is to stop breathing and panic over rapid change, which is why people begin to hyperventilate when they get stressed out. Deep breathing overcomes that tendency. And after taking that deep breath, reflect. *Let me see; what just happened?*

Then study the environment, so that you'll know how to properly respond, rather than react. Response always requires thought. Most people simply react, which requires little thought, and in a panic situation they'll inevitably make terrible, grave mistakes.

So *be aware.* And to promote that awareness, remind yourself to pause, breathe, reflect, and study your environment.

Take Action

Master change by taking appropriate action.

Spiritually, this means upgrading your prayer life and your Bible reading. The Word of God is filled with incredible answers, if we're sensitive to hear the voice of God through the ministry of His Spirit bringing life to the Word of God. The Lord will speak to you and impart to you the wisdom and understanding you need for this very moment. Upgrade not only your prayer life and your Bible reading, but also your information—because your judgment is no better than your information. Get the facts.

DON'T *KILL* YOURSELF; *SKILL* YOURSELF.

Upgrade also your skills or your certifications in particular areas. When the economy is changing, and the job market is changing, you've got to become more marketable, more useable. Don't kill yourself; *skill* yourself. Become more hirable. Or, if you're entering a new stage of life such as parenthood, educate yourself. Find books or resources by respected Christians on how to be a great, godly parent.

Remember also that you were built to learn new things. Don't buy into the lie that you can't teach an old dog new tricks. Have you actually ever tried to teach new tricks to an old dog? If you reward him with enough little snacks, old Spot will learn how to roll over, sit, or heel. Oh yes, you can teach him!

I heard recently of a lady who's seventy-four years old and runs ten miles a day. She didn't even start running until she was fifty-something! So don't dare say you can't do something new because you're getting too old! Don't let anybody else put a label on you; you have to be careful when you're around lots of low-achieving or negative people. Don't let them influence your view of yourself, and don't let them keep you from taking the action you know is right.

Taking the right action also means getting enough exercise, enough sleep, and the right food in the right quantities. Often when we're facing big changes, we start ignoring all those things, making us irritable and hard to live with. Even *you* find yourself hard to live with. So, however obvious this may seem, do what it takes to keep well-rested, to get refreshed and strengthened through exercise, and to stay nourished with good nutrition.

As a side note here, I also encourage you to find humor wherever you can. There's plenty in this world that makes you want to cry, so you've got to consciously look for what will make you laugh. Laughter lowers your blood pressure and relieves stress. It's amazing to learn of the physical benefits that can come from a good laugh, as studies have shown.[1]

So take action; turn your fears and anxieties into positive activity. And by *action*, I mean *new and different actions*. Show by your actions how you're repositioning yourself. If there was ever a time to reposition yourself, that time is now, because whatever got you where you are right now—your past training, the technology of the past, or whatever—will *not* get you where you want to go in the future.

As you face an environment of profound change, you may have the desire to take action, but yet hardly know where to begin. You simply can't solve everything all at once and you're practically paralyzed by the scope of what's before you. If that's your situation, then I suggest breaking down that immense difficulty into smaller components. Once you start working out one small thing and solving one small part of the problem, you'll be surprised—every small solution opens the door to a bigger one. So just get into a problem-solving mode and simplify your approach. If there are twenty-five things that need correcting or adjusting, just start with three. This will create momentum, and there's real power in just getting started and getting a few things done. That momentum will bless your life.

---

1. See "Stress Management," Mayo Clinic, www.mayoclinic.org/healthy-living/stress-management/in-depth/stress-relief/art-20044456 (accessed 22 April 2015).

Stay Connected

Master change by staying connected with people, not by avoiding them in a grand old pity party. Get around people and talk with them; don't become isolated. See what you can learn from them.

I've mentioned this concept before, but I want to explain it a little better now: I see every person as a *treasure*. There's gold in everybody, but it has to be mined. Sometimes you have to push through some dirt in order to get to the gold. I don't allow the dirtiness that I might see in people—whether it's the filthiness of their language, the destitution of their lives, or the apparent arrogance of their hearts, or whatever it might be—to hide the fact that there's great value in every human being, something that they can teach you and me. I've heard some absolutely great wisdom come out of the mouths of people who are living out on the street. You would be surprised how much brilliance is possessed by people who've been rejected by society. See yourself as being on a treasure hunt as you interact with all kinds of people; seek and you shall find.

THE FURTHER BACK YOU LOOK, THE FURTHER AHEAD YOU CAN SEE.

Treasure is typically hidden, so you have to talk with people, observe them at length, and get to know them carefully and deeply. Everything that a person has been through and the lessons they've learned can become *your* wisdom if you learn how to mine the treasure out of them. Don't have the attitude that you know it all. Cultivate relational humility, recognizing that you can learn something from anyone. Recognize the value of the varied perspectives others can offer you.

If you're old, stay connected with younger people. They'll help you to understand the culture of change, because they embrace today's changes more easily. They can serve as your tour guide in helping you to adjust. They're often naturally skilled in the kinds of things that you find hard to get accustomed to. So stay connected with them, and you'll become energized by them.

And if you're young, stay connected with older people. Yeah, you might think they're boring, but whatever you're going through right now, there's a pretty good chance that they've gone through it, too. Let me just tell you this, young folks, the further back you look, the further ahead you can see. There's a wisdom in your grandparents, and in your great grandparents, that you don't yet possess. Younger people think everything is new, but old folks know there's nothing new under the sun. Stay connected with them, and you'll be matured by them.

Everybody needs at least three vital relationships in their life. First, everybody needs a Paul. Paul was a father, a mentor. He could show you how to live, how to do missions; he could teach you the ropes. He blazed the trail and left it open for the rest of us to follow.

Second, everybody needs a Barnabas. The name Barnabas means "encourager," and everybody needs an encourager. Every husband needs an encourager in his wife; men need a cheerleader who will cheer even when he's losing the game. When a man least deserves love, that's when he needs it the most. And when a woman has messed up, she needs a Barnabas, too! She doesn't need a judge; she doesn't need a coach yelling in her face, "What were you doing! What were you thinking! Did you lose your mind?" She needs somebody who will be tender and compassionate, who will honor her and respect her, who will assure her, "You're still my babe...." This Barnabas relationship is somebody who's not so infatuated with you that they can't tell you the truth about yourself. They're not stuck on your image. They can be honest with you and shoot from the hip in order to make you better.

Third, everybody needs a Timothy. Timothy is the mentee, the protégé that the mentor pours into. After you've had people pour into you, learn how to pour into others. Somebody helped you, so you ought now to help others. Give them the benefit of your wisdom. Share your knowledge with them. Notice that at different times you can be all three—you can be somebody's Paul, their Barnabas, and their Timothy. Regardless of what your exact relationship is, however, just be sure to connect with people.

Learn from Every Change

Master change by learning from it, so that you're better prepared for the next wave. First find out what caused the change, then ask if it could have been avoided; if it could not have been avoided, then ask why the change is genuinely necessary. Anticipate future change, and decide how to influence it instead of how to be a victim to it. What can you be doing already, right here, right now, to initiate helpful change?

← DON'T JUST **GO** THROUGH LIFE; **GROW** THROUGH LIFE. →

You're divinely designed to be a learner. God has strategically made us with so much precision, but also with much flexibility. The good news of the gospel is that you don't have to stay in the place where you are! Remember that your future is not based on where you are; it is based on where you decide to stay.

Be flexible in the midst of change, but also locate and identify your *constants* and your *variables*. There must be an anchor that secures you, so that you can say, "This is who I am. This is where I belong right now." Find your anchor, find your principles that never change. Find those elements that should never change—your non-negotiables. And if you don't have any, you better start searching Jesus' Word for some right now!

Don't just *go* through life; *grow* through life. Strive to be open and flexible to change. The mighty oak tree will break amid a storm, but a flexible palm tree will bend to the ground, and when the storm has passed it will rise back up again. Be like that palm tree, ready for whatever hurricane comes your way on the seascape of today's world.

And remember that the answers are always changing—something that may have been true last year is not necessarily true this year. Let me share with you a revealing anecdote from the life of the great physicist Albert Einstein.

The story is told about how Einstein and a teaching assistant were walking back to the professor's office after he had administered an exam to an advanced class of physics students. With the test papers stacked in his arms, the assistant asked, "Dr. Einstein, wasn't this the same exam you gave these same students last year?"

The professor answered that indeed it was.

The young assistant continued, "Excuse me for asking, sir, but how could you give them the same exam two years in a row?"

Einstein looked at his assistant and responded, "Son, the answers have changed."[2]

WHINERS ARE NOT WINNERS AND WINNERS ARE NOT WHINERS.

Yes, so many answers to our questions are not what they used to be! There are many things that worked fine in years past, but now our culture has changed—and so have the answers and the solutions and the best approaches.

Avoid Complaining

Complaining is the hallmark of a victim, not a master. Complaining nails you to your problems; complaining attracts negative situations

2. See "Albert Einstein Anecdotes," The Gold Scales, http://oaks.nvg.org/sa5ra17.html (accessed 22 April 2015).

and negative people to you. Whiners are not winners and winners are not whiners. Did you know that the children of Israel wandered in the wilderness for forty years until a whole generation passed away because God couldn't take their complaining? They did nothing but complain, gripe, and belly-ache—about everything that they thought was going wrong. *"Then the whole congregation of the children of Israel complained against Moses and Aaron in the wilderness…. 'Oh, that we had died by the hand of the Lord in the land of Egypt, when we sat by the pots of meat and when we ate bread to the full! For you have brought us out into this wilderness to kill this whole assembly with hunger'"* (Exodus 16:2–3).

Have you noticed that complaining doesn't make things better, but rather worse? Have you ever seen chronic complainers fix their problems by complaining? Complaining is like tying your own hands behind your back and expecting someone else to free you! Instead of complaining, ask questions. Seek understanding. Think, *Why did this go wrong? Did I contribute to this? Did I have the wrong timing? Did I have the wrong motives? What does God want me to learn from this? What can I do better next time?*

No doubt about it, there are uncomfortable things that will happen when you're in transition. You will feel like complaining. You will get tired of eating the same old thing every day, and walking in the same old sandals, like the Israelites. But transitions aren't designed to be comfortable! The Israelites cried out to God to take them back to the good old days in Egypt where they had lots of fresh fruits and veggies, meats and spices. But they forgot one thing: back in Egypt, what were they? Kings? Servants? No, they were *slaves!*

So when we start asking God to "take us back, back to the good ole days," be truthful and honest with yourself: it wasn't all that good back there! There was so much you didn't have. God is trying to take us to a brand-new place: the best is yet to come. I'm telling you, it just gets better. Heaven is in front of us, not behind us.

I've had bad days, too—we all have. I'm not denying that things can be terribly rough. But I've had good days too, and I won't complain.

No, as long as there is breath in my body, I will bless my Lord. Naked I came into this world, and naked am I going to go out; blessed be the name of the Lord. I refuse to be known as a complainer. I don't want anybody to see me walk in the door and say, "Oh, here he comes again—watch out! He's about to complain. 'The food was too salty. It was too spicy. It was too hot. It was too cold. It cost too much. It was too cheap. It had too much fat on it.'" Those kind of people will find something wrong with everything. And their attitudes are contagious.

When I ask people how they are doing and they say, "Well I can't complain," I say, "Well, it wouldn't help if you did." To be a master of change, abstain from complaining. Address negative things, but don't dwell on them. Have a thirty-second rule—thirty seconds to say what's wrong, and then you're done. Then the sun comes out again.

7

Your Thought Life

We cannot live above the level of our thinking. Each of us is limited to the knowledge that's in our mind, as well as the perspectives and assumptions that fill and color our thoughts. You'll never be in the future any more than what you can *think* you are right now. Each person is truly defined by what's happening inside him mentally: "*As he thinketh in his heart, so is he*" (Proverbs 23:7 KJV). Your life is limited to the level of your thinking.

← **WE CANNOT LIVE ABOVE THE LEVEL OF OUR THINKING.** →

My dad started thinking of himself as a millionaire before he ever was. He started out his business with $17.42 in his pocket, but he thought of himself as a millionaire. If you knew that his bank account could fit inside the head of needle, you would have thought he was crazy, the way he carried himself! But nobody on the street knew his bank account; they just saw a man who carried himself confidently and carefully. Folks thought he was a millionaire while he was still living paycheck by paycheck, simply because he conducted himself like one.

As your life experiences change, you must change your thinking. You've got to *rethink*. You can't mentally process things the same way you always have. As your life experiences evolve, your thinking must evolve along with them. Albert Einstein once said, "The significant problems that we face cannot be solved at the same level of thinking we were at when we created them."[3] So we have to change our thought patterns and our mental approaches.

In this chapter I want to direct your attention to a few specific skills and practices that can help you to raise your level of *thinking*—of your thought life. Think of these skills as doorways that lead to a higher level of thinking.

Reevaluate Your New Reality

When you go through change, stop and reevaluate. You'll know it's time to reevaluate your life when you start experiencing stress, resistance, frustration, failure, disappointment, or difficulties of any kind. Could that be you right now?

If you're chronically irritable, angry, or unhappy with your work or your personal situation, there's a cognitive dissonance between where you *are* and where you know you *should be*. If that's what you're experiencing, don't be discouraged. If you realize, "I'm getting older, I'm not happy, I'm frustrated, I'm stressed," then stop and consider *what* you're doing, *why* you're doing it, *when* you're doing it, and *who* you're doing it for and with.

Anytime things have shifted and moved, you've got to find out, "Where am I right now?" Whenever you're dealing with change, your first responsibility is to define reality. You've got to get the facts. You can't change reality until you accurately define it. See the world as it is, not as you wish it to be. You can't base your plans merely on where you *think* you are; you've got to find out where you *really* are, and base your plans on that. You've got to recognize reality and deal with reality.

3. "Albert Einstein Quotes," Albert Einstein Site, www.alberteinsteinsite.com/quotes/einsteinquotes (accessed 22 April 2015).

Remember that the current reality is most likely a *new* reality, not the past reality that you've grown accustomed to.

Before you can continue on successfully to your destination, you'll need to recalibrate. In your positioning system, the satellite has got to find out where you currently are, or else it can't give you directions as to where you need to be. That's why you need to reevaluate.

SEE THE WORLD AS IT IS, NOT AS YOU WISH IT TO BE.

If you really want an objective evaluation, ask your neighbor. Ask your friend. Ask somebody who's close to you, who's not infatuated with you, and who will tell you the truth about yourself. If your friends are just telling you flattering things, then they're not really being friends. The Bible says that we ought to *provoke* one another unto love and good works. We all need that kind of provocation. You need the truth. You need an honest evaluation.

So whenever you find yourself in pain, in turmoil, in frustration, or in depression, your mind is doing battle with itself. Listen to the battle, listen to your thoughts. Verbalize. Reevaluate. Ask yourself some serious questions, like: What parts of my life need reorganizing or restructuring, in light of my new reality? How can I be more effective and more efficient in pressing toward my true goal in life? What needs to be simplified in my life, to reduce the complexity and the strain? You may soon realize that there's a way to align the *where you are* with the *where you should be.*

Put It on Paper

When you're processing change, ask these questions and then write down your best answers. To sharpen and deepen your thinking about any particular situation that burdens and stresses you, simply write down the details of it on a piece of paper. The more details you write down, the calmer, clearer, and more effective your thinking will become. Very often, the right course of action will actually seem to jump off the page when you take time to write down these details the old-fashioned way.

As you write, include as much detail as possible. Instead of wrestling with all those multiple factors as they churn in your mind, instead of getting frustrated, instead of losing sleep as you toss and turn and fret over these things, just get everything down on paper where you can calmly and clearly examine the situation and decide how to deal with it. Put a pad of paper next to your bed, so if you're wrestling with something through the night, you can write it down.

Here's the principle: *On the paper, out of the mind.* You can manage the situation better when its details are spelled out in ink right in front of you than when they're raging randomly through your brain. On paper, you can organize the details, analyze them, and compartmentalize them. It will help you see where there might be a breakdown and where things need to change. You'll be surprised how this will help steer your thoughts toward a valid solution.

Be Willing to Reinvent Yourself

Reinventing yourself involves drawing a line under your past and imagining what you could or should do in starting over today with a clean slate. Ask yourself this question: If my home and my business burned to the ground overnight, and I had to start all over again— what would I do differently? What would I start back up immediately, and what would I never start up again? What would I replace? What would I update? What would I try to keep the same as before?

Just thinking through that exercise can spawn ideas for what you can strategically accomplish right now—without having to lose anything in a fire!

Here's another good line of questioning: If your field of expertise, your career area, became obsolete, and those skills and abilities were no longer wanted by anyone, what new type of work would you choose? If you had to start all over again, *where* would you choose to do it? What skills or abilities would you choose to develop or to refine? How would you reinvent yourself?

Companies that don't innovate don't survive. In fact, the more successful a company is, the more it has to innovate in order to stay on top. Those who don't innovate end up being overtaken or displaced by those that do. If you have a business that doesn't innovate, or a ministry that doesn't innovate, it will become irrelevant. And individuals who don't innovate or reposition themselves will similarly find themselves out of a position, out of influence, and out of touch. So keep changing yourself and keep challenging yourself.

This will mean you have to constantly confront your limitations, and refuse to be average. Nobody's going out of their way to hire average people. Businesses want exceptional people to work for them, so don't be average. You have to be forward-thinking. You have to look realistically at the changing seascape where we all find ourselves, learn all you can, and respond to that.

And don't forget that this is a task for *you*, not for anybody else. You must be willing to be like an eagle, soaring in loneliness but also grandeur. We're not called to be in all of these clusters and cliques of people who make us feel great about ourselves because they're just like us. If God's going to develop you and take you to the next level, you won't be going there with a whole group of friends. When God's taking you through something, your friends can't go through it with you. Your spouse can't go through it with you. Your best friend, or sister, or brother, or son, or daughter, can't. If you are called to do anything of any significance, you must be acquainted with loneliness.

Work on Yourself

Make a note of this: Work harder on *yourself* than you do on your job. Think of yourself as multitalented. Have a mind-set of both excellence and versatility.

Training at work allows you to perform a particular job, but developing yourself as a person allows you to do *many* kinds of jobs. So develop and train yourself in various areas, and you'll make yourself more valuable. If your workplace were to cut employees, you'll more easily find an open door elsewhere because you've developed yourself.

By telling you to work harder on yourself than you do on your job, I'm not talking about shortchanging the present position where you work. The truth is, when you work harder on *yourself*, you end up becoming more valuable in *any* job, including your present one. Sometimes companies have complained about how often they see an employee leave after they had invested money and training in that person. But as others have observed, it's worse to *not* train them and have them stay!

WORK HARDER *ON YOURSELF* THAN YOU DO *ON YOUR JOB*.

A principal overheard a teacher telling somebody that she had twenty-five years of experience in teaching. That principal later commented, "This woman does not have twenty-five years of teaching experience; she has *one* year of experience that's been repeated twenty-five times!" There's a huge difference! The principal had observed that this woman never took the time to develop herself. She felt that she'd already learned her position, and that's all she planned to give to it. She wasn't giving it any more than she already had. And because of that, she was missing out—and so were her students.

You make a terrible mistake in your life when you just learn the role in your position and never develop yourself to become more. When you develop yourself to become better, you're worth more in the place where you are, and you create greater doors of opportunity for yourself in many other places.

We ought to start a campaign: "Stop the mediocrity!" It's time that you get fed up with doing just enough to get by, just enough to keep from getting fired. Instead say, "I want something different; I want to have *an excellent spirit* within me, in everything I do, in every area of life." That resolution begins in your thoughts and quickly percolates into every other area of your life.

8

Your Vision

Vision is a picture of the future—how things can be and how things should be. Only you can know exactly what your vision is. Vision, literally, is the ability to see the ground in front of you. But, metaphorically, it means even more; it means the ability to see where life may take you, where certain decisions will lead you, what certain people might do for you. It gives you that picture of the future which you desire so much. It shows you what your life *can* be and what it *should* be. If you're missing that vision—if you don't know how things ought to be for you—then you won't be able to take the practical steps.

WHERE VISION IS LACKING, PEOPLE PERISH.

In order to change from where you are, you've got to decide where you'd rather be. You've got to see yourself in another place, operating on another level, doing things differently. There's nothing more powerful than getting a picture of your future that will cause you to be pregnant with purpose and give birth to action.

Where there's no vision, what happens? The book of Proverbs tells us: "*Where there is no vision, the people perish*" (Proverbs 29:18 KJV). Creating a vision for your life should demand your full attention.

Believing Is Seeing

Do you realize that it was only after Abraham got a picture of his future that he had sufficient faith to bring into manifestation what God told him was going to happen to him? God had commanded this man to get up and go to the land He would show him, and God promised him that there He would make him the father of many nations. Abraham was hearing these amazing things, things he had never seen or imagined.

Now recall that one starry night when Abraham had already pitched his tent in this new land where he had been led, and God brought him outside his tent and spoke to Abraham: *"Look now toward heaven, and count the stars if you are able to number them....So shall your descendants be"* (Genesis 15:5). God was showing him something, giving him a picture. Then immediately we read this about Abraham: *"And he believed in the LORD, and He accounted it to him for righteousness"* (15:6). God gave Abraham a picture, and nine months later his son Isaac was born—the son of promise. After that, in his new faith, Abraham would go on to father Isaac and the nation of Israel.

Abraham believed! Faith is seeing as Abraham saw: beyond tangible reality into the promises of the future. To have faith, you've got to see something; if you cannot see it by faith, you'll never get it. You must envision it, as you trust in God. Until what God has said to you becomes visible within your mind and heart, it will never happen. You've first got to get a picture of it.

Maybe you've heard yourself say, "I just can't see myself doing such and such." Well, if that's true—if you can't see yourself doing that thing—you'll never do it. There's something that causes faith to spring up the moment you can see it. That's why we need vision of the heavenly kind.

Scientific researchers have done experiments with the human mind, and they've discovered that the mind cannot tell the difference between what is imaginary and what is real. That's why when you're asleep and you're having an action-packed dream, your body doesn't know it's a dream; your heart rate accelerates, your breathing gets faster, and you start perspiring. If somebody's chasing you in your dream, it's as if they really are chasing you. Your mind doesn't know the difference.

In the same way, when God shows you a vision of something on the inside, everything in your system begins to line up and act as though it is actual reality. Remember again these words of promise that God gives His people: *"For I know the plans I have for you, declares the LORD, plans for welfare and not for evil, to give you a future and a hope"* (Jeremiah 29:11 ESV). Yes, God has plans for you; in that same passage, He goes on to say:

> *Then you will call upon Me and go and pray to Me, and I will listen to you. And you will seek Me and find Me, when you search for Me with all your heart. I will be found by you, says the LORD.*
> (verses 12–14)

God is saying, "When you seek Me with all your heart, I'll tell you what these plans are. I want you to get a picture of them." It's the Word of the Lord that brings this picture into our hearts—because words create images. So listen to the Word of the Lord!

You have to get a picture of it. You don't become empowered until you can see this thing as happening to *you*. You almost have to talk yourself into it, to where you believe this thing. The picture comes into sharper focus as God begins to show you the love He has for you, and the joy He has for you, and the peace of mind, and how He wants to use you. Can you believe that God can let this miracle power flow through your life and through your words and through your hands?

Vision Brings Discipline

With true vision from the Lord, you can finally see a way out of your present predicament. If you want something you've never had, you've got to do something you've never done—because if you keep on doing what you've always done, you'll keep on getting what you've always gotten.

REPEATING THE PAST ONLY CREATES MORE OF THE PAST.

I want you to realize this very carefully: Repeating the past won't create a new future; repeating the past only creates more of the past. To leave from where you are, you must decide where you would rather be, and make the changes necessary to get there. And the real key is that all this requires vision, a picture of the future. That's what vision is all about.

Once you have that clear vision, you've got the motivation to really pursue some new things with energy and diligence. Vision brings discipline in your life. You're disciplined because you know you're working toward something meaningful and productive.

Without that understanding, people's lives run amok. Remember the Scripture that says, *"Where there is no vision the people perish"*? Another version translates it, *"Where there is no vision, the people are unrestrained"* (Proverbs 29:18 NASB); others translate it as *"people are uncontrolled"* (NCV) and *"people run wild"* (GW). Undisciplined people are unrestrained, uncontrolled, and running wild—because they have no vision.

Vision Promotes Planning, Preparation, and Expectation

True vision not only brings discipline, it also promotes planning, which in turn builds expectation. Your vision is a picture of the future and how things can be and should be, and that should make you excited and eager. I love what Zig Ziglar says: "You were born to win, but to be a winner, you must plan to win, prepare to win, and expect to win." Winning is never an accident; you have to get ready for it.

If you're going to win in this next stage and season of your life, it won't happen automatically. It takes planning, preparation, and expectation. You've got to expect certain things—the right things. Don't expect the world to be nice to you. You know what disappointment is? Disappointment is the distance between what you expect and the reality of what you get. When you've got this unrealistic expectation that everybody's going to love you, pat you on the back, encourage you, and make your path easy for you, then reality will bring you a big dose of disappointment. The greater your expectations, and the lesser the actual reality, the bigger your disappointment will be.

The truth is that there will always be some folks ready to talk negatively about us, to question our motives and methods and abilities. But if we realize ahead of time that this is just what people always tend to do, we'll narrow the gap of any disappointment over that. I'm not talking about lowering our expectation of God, but about lowering our expectations of the world's system, which is anti-God.

If you've got vision, you're able to say, "God, I am more than what others say I am." That's why you should never let anybody else make your world for you, because they'll always create it too small! So as God shows you a vision for the future, you've got to be planning and preparing for a changing trajectory. Only those who plan for that, prepare for it, and expect it will ultimately be successful. When the vision comes and grows—as God allows you to see something good that He's showing you toward your future—that's His way of saying, "Prepare your heart, and prepare your mind. I want you to prepare, even before you can understand how this will all work out."

Think about how the root meaning of *provision* is "foreseeing"— looking ahead and seeing needs before you have them. Provision springs from vision. You have to plan ahead because it wasn't raining when Noah built the ark. If you wait until it's raining to build something, you're too late. Noah didn't wait for his ship to come in; he built one. God had to really change his trajectory because Noah didn't even know about rain—prior to the flood, it had never rained on the earth. The Bible says that there was a mist that came up from the ground that watered the earth, but it had never rained. Nobody had ever seen precipitation fall from a cloud. So God gave Noah a vision, and he planned—for years—while his neighbors laughed at him up and down. But who got the last laugh there?

NOAH DIDN'T WAIT FOR HIS SHIP TO COME IN; HE BUILT ONE.

Get Beyond Complacency and Stagnation

I want you to notice something from the first chapter of the book of Zephaniah, where Zephaniah is prophesying to Judah about judgment that's coming upon those who think nothing's going to change in the future. The Lord God gives them this message:

> *It shall come to pass at that time that I will search Jerusalem with lamps, and punish the men who are settled in complacency, who say in their heart, "The LORD will not do good, nor will He do evil."*   (Zephaniah 1:12)

This is a prophetic message to God's people letting us know that things aren't going to stay the same as they've always been. Not only is it incorrect to think that things won't change—it's a downright sin! Conditions will continue to get stirred up and to evolve. And when you live today as though nothing will ever change in the future—it will cause you to never *prepare* for the future.

You'll be *"settled in complacency,"* as this verse says. In the way these words are translated in other Scripture versions, such people are described as *"stagnant in spirit"* (NASB); they're people *"who settle down* comfortably" (HCSB); or as *The Message* paraphrases it, *"those who are sitting it out, fat and lazy, amusing themselves and taking it easy."*

You don't want to be complacent in unstable, uncertain times like these. You really don't want to be stagnant and settled into comfort. Those who have settled into complacency, who are stagnant in spirit, who refuse to change—they're the ones singing, "I shall not, I shall not be moved." Well sometimes if you don't move, you'll get run over. The environment is still changing around you, and if *you* don't change, you might think you're holding your own, but you're actually slipping back. You're losing ground and failing to make progress. It's impossible to stay in one place: you're either *progressing* or you're *regressing*.

SOMETIMES IF YOU DON'T MOVE, YOU'LL GET RUN OVER.

To stay stuck in the place where you are—mentally, emotionally, psychologically—is like living under a curse. Perhaps you've encountered old friends and classmates from your school days who, as you chat together, reveal by their attitudes and conversation that they are still in the same place mentally and emotionally as they were back in school. You can tell it by the way they treat you; since *they* haven't changed, they assume *you* haven't changed. So they're stuck in the place where they are. And that is bad news.

If you've made no preparation to move forward into the future, you'll be relegated to where you are. Twenty years down the road, you'll be thinking the same way you're thinking now, with the same old habits and limitations. When you keep on doing the same things the same way, you'll continue to get the same results, and nothing better. Do you know people who are satisfied with their hardened lifestyle? They don't feel like they need to change, and they're telling folks, "I'm grown; I'll do what I want." Whenever you get to the place of thinking God won't do anything, and you can live as you please and get away with it—that's a dangerous deception. Such people will get caught in God's punishment with their works undone, and their calling unfulfilled.

9

Your Future

There's a Latino proverb that says, "Un hombre no está donde el está, pero donde ama." It translates to, "A man is not where he lives; he is where he loves." What is the destination that you love, that God has given you a vision for? Are you looking ahead to that?

One characteristic of the most successful and happiest people is that they're intensely future-oriented. They refuse to dwell on what has happened in the past, on the things that cannot be changed. Instead, they focus on the factors that are under their control and the actions they can take in order to create the kind of future they desire. They believe their best days and their most satisfying experiences actually lie in the future, waiting to be created and enjoyed. They look toward the future like a child looks to Christmas.

But why would anybody who's gone through pain—and I'd bet my bottom dollar that every last one of us has—be excited about the future? The answer is pretty simple: because we're not made to live in *comfort*, we're made to live with *purpose*. I love something that Harvard business professor Rosabeth Moss-Kanter once wrote about purpose: "To stay ahead, you must have your next idea waiting in the wings." And that next idea for your life will be fully on display in the vision God gives you, as you wait for Him and seek Him. We've talked much about the uncertainty and discomfort that come with change. But the fact is, change can be good—very good. There are *personal* changes you're going through now, as well as ones that you'll experience later, that are not only good, they're *necessary*.

Anything with real life *grows*. That's the greatest sign that something is alive—when it's actually growing. *You* ought to be growing. I don't care how old you are, your thoughts and emotions and perspectives ought to be expanding and maturing into the future.

Write a Mission Statement

To focus on your purpose as you look to the future, I want to encourage you to write a mission statement for the rest of your life. A personal mission statement answers three basic questions.

1. What is my life about?

2. What do I stand for?

3. What action am I taking to live out what my life is about and what I stand for?

Ask yourself those three questions. Make sure to make your mission statement congruent with who you *are*—right here, right now. That's the exact person that God wants to use. Don't try to be somebody that you're not. Be *yourself*. There'll be one word that people associate with your name. Just one word. When you think of Job, people immediately say, "The patience of Job." They think about patience. When they think about Abraham, they think about faith. When they think about Moses, they think about meekness. When I say, "Tiger Woods," you think, *golf*. When I say, "Serena Williams," you think, *tennis*. What will your word be?

What I am changes, but who I am matters eternally. Never allow the *what* to confuse the *who*. Never allow your circumstances confuse to who you're supposed to be. I'm not suggesting that it will be easy to answer these questions. Separating who you actually are from what role you're in can be extremely difficult because the one influences the other dramatically. But sometimes the Lord has something for you to do that requires you to really ask who you actually are. Jacob wrestled with an angel because he was just that desperate for an answer to his persistent question: *Who am I, Lord, and what am I supposed to do?* He just had no idea. And the Lord blessed his struggle by providing an answer.

WHAT I AM CHANGES, BUT *WHO* I AM MATTERS ETERNALLY.

Let me remind you of the wonderful guy years ago by the name of Sir Alfred who woke up one morning, sat at his breakfast table, and opened up his newspaper. He read the obituaries, and saw his own name in big black print! His obituary had been printed by mistake; the newspaper had confused Sir Alfred with his recently deceased brother. So Sir Alfred read his obituary over a nice cup of coffee, and he was not proud of what he read. The obituary went on and on about how this man, Sir Alfred, had discovered of TNT dynamite which had wreaked destruction all over the world, destroying things and places and so many people's lives. Sir Alfred sat up straight in his nice wooden chair. He wasn't proud of what had made him rich in his life and how he was being remembered. It made him stop and ask, *how do I want to be remembered?* He made a decision that day—a firm, unwavering decision—and changed his trajectory and his destiny. Today, we don't know him merely as Sir Alfred. His name is Sir Alfred Nobel—the founder of the Nobel Peace Prize. He is no longer known for the destruction that, in some way, he caused through discovering dynamite. He's known for peace.

You, too, have the ability to change how you are remembered. Whatever it is that you're dealing with in your life today, you have the ability to stop and say, "Lord, what am I actually called to do?" When you find a young man or young woman who is driven by vision and purpose, their lives don't get off track into all kinds of aberrant misbe-haviors. It's only where there is no vision that people perish.

GOD CREATED YOU ON PURPOSE, WITH PURPOSE, FOR PURPOSE.

God put that energy in you and that creative mind, and if you're not working on positive purpose, you'll use it for something that is demonic and satanic—destructive in its behavior toward you and oth-ers. That's why the best thing that you can do for yourself or a young person in your life is to connect them with their God-purpose.

Every man, every woman, is living a dry, dull, and insipid life doing mundane, boring, and routine things until they come alive in their purpose. God knows exactly why He created you. And He didn't create you to be just like anybody else because, if that were the case, one of you is unnecessary. God created you on purpose, with purpose, for purpose, and until you tap into that purpose, you won't really come alive. You're not an accident. You're not just some protoplasm that showed up out of the sea and took on form by mor-phing over ages of time. You were created as an intentional divine creation of God; you were placed in the earth to fill a need and to solve a problem. I challenge you today to have a hunger toward God to say, "God, why am I here? I know that I'm put here for more than just inhaling and exhaling and paying taxes."

Arise and Be Remade

The changes needed in your life may sometimes call for a totally new start in a certain area. In fact, that's often the case. Some people are of the opinion that if you're in God's hands, you'll never have to start over with anything. But I want to show you from the Word of God that you can be in the Lord's hand and still get in bad shape. It doesn't mean you're no longer in His hands, and it doesn't mean you're not His child. But it does mean He wants you to make some huge adjustments.

At the beginning of Jeremiah 18, the Lord's word to His prophet begins like this: *"Arise…."* You know what that word *arise* means? *Get up and go to a higher level!* You'll never go anyplace in life until you arise like that, in mind as well as body.

In this encounter with Jeremiah, God told him, *"Arise and go down to the potter's house"* (Jeremiah 18:2). Jeremiah obeyed, and went to the house of the potter:

> *And there he was, making something at the wheel. And the vessel that he made of clay was **marred** in the hand of the potter; so he made it again into another vessel, as it seemed good to the potter to make.* (verses 3–4)

The word *marred* here means "messed up, disfigured;" the clay vessel was flawed and defective. The Lord then interpreted this sight for Jeremiah: *"Then the word of the LORD came to me, saying: 'O house of Israel, can I not do with you as this potter?' says the LORD. 'Look, as the clay is in the potter's hand, so are you in My hand, O house of Israel!'"* (verses 5–6).

The potter had to remake the clay vessel that got messed up in his own hand; he was obliged to form it into a new vessel. He had to reinvent it. He had to refashion it, redesign it, and create it into a new container altogether.

The church today is the new, spiritual Israel, and God is saying, "Listen, church, you've gotten messed up. Even though you were in My hand, you have been marred, and I'm getting ready to shape you into a brand new vessel." I'm so glad that God honors His Word—not just sometimes, but all the time. It's impossible for Him to lie. If God spoke of something that did not yet exist, it would have to come into being in that moment, because God cannot lie. He will be faithful to these incredible promises.

For some, He causes the road to traverse the wilderness; He causes the river to stream forth in the desert. Maybe you're a child of God whose credit is all jacked up. Being in that awful situation doesn't mean you're not a child of God. It just means you need a fresh start in how you handle your finances. Please understand that if your credit is in shambles, it's not because of God. God didn't run up your debts. But He can help you start over.

IF YOU'RE ON A ROAD THAT'S NOT LEADING ANYWHERE—TRAVEL ANOTHER ROAD!

God is all about making things new. "*Therefore, if anyone is in Christ, he is a new creation; old things have passed away; behold, **all things have become new**" (2 Corinthians 5:17). God wants to make us into a brand new vessel; He's saying, "I'm going to put a new mindset in you." It's like giving a computer an entirely new operating system. When you're operating with an old system, there are certain programs that you just can't run; until you change that system, you won't get any new results. For many different reasons, we can get messed up while we're in His hand. But God says, "I'll make you into another vessel, a vessel of honor, a vessel I can use in new ways. I've got to show you how to be flexible and adaptable for all that, so you can be useful for many things." So God makes you into something that you were not before.

God Will Make a Way—a *New* Way

God has said He will do *a new thing*. He's committed to that:

Do not remember the former things, nor consider the things of old. Behold, I will do a new thing, now it shall spring forth; shall you not know it? I will even make a road in the wilderness and rivers in the desert.   (Isaiah 43:18–19)

He's saying, "I'm going to do some things you haven't heard of before; I'm going to do some things for you that you've not yet seen. I'm going to defy logic and common sense, for I'm going to make a road *in the wilderness,* and rivers *in the desert.*

Oh, the awesomeness of our wonderful, wonderful God! Here is a new highway for us. If you're on a road that's not leading anywhere—travel another road! And that's what God offers us. The wilderness is the place where no one travels, but God is building a road there; the desert is where nothing grows, only barren dryness, but God says He'll make life-giving rivers there.

So God says, "I'm getting ready to do some things...and it's all *to make a way for you.*" God will make a way for you; somehow, He'll make a way. You don't always know how and when it's coming, but you do know that God will make a way. *"Behold,"* He says, *"I will do a new thing."* At times, the thing He does may seem only a small something that He's giving to us—but you can go a long way with it!

PART THREE:

Getting Practical

10

10 Principles for Changing Your Trajectory

You'll notice that you're only half-way through this book, but you're already on the final part, *Getting Practical*. Why? Because practical help is what I'm here to give you. Theoretical sounds great, and when you read it, it feels great, but when it comes to waking up tomorrow morning and stumbling out of bed, you need more than theory. You need practical steps, so that when you look in the mirror, you can say, "Remember? Remember what you have to do?"

So here are ten practical steps. Ten principles for changing your trajectory. Ten changeless truths to return to again and again. Remember, principles never change—policies and procedures do, but principles don't.

Principle #1: Seek the Lord

When it's time to change your trajectory, *seek the Lord*. Don't do anything without consulting Him. Don't make major moves without checking with God.

Let's listen again to the promises of God in Jeremiah 29, this time as paraphrased in *The Message*:

I know what I'm doing. I have it all planned out—plans to take care of you, not abandon you, plans to give you the future you hope for. When you call on me, when you come and pray to me, I'll listen. When you come looking for me, you'll find me. Yes, when you get serious about finding me and want it more than anything else, I'll make sure you won't be disappointed.... I'll turn things around for you...You can count on it. (verses 11–14)

If you seek Him, God will say to you, "I'm glad you've come looking for Me! I'm so glad you're calling on Me! And I'm *listening!*" He will respond by speaking to your mind and heart with multiple assurances of His plans and His presence and with a vision for your future. By faith you'll be able to count on the fact that things will turn around for you.

← TAKE GOD AT HIS WORD. →

So seek and ask—ask and it shall be given. Take God at His word. Find His will.

When you know it's time to change your trajectory, say to Him, "Lord, where am I supposed to go now?" Wisdom is simply knowing what to do next. If you don't know what to do next, *ask the Lord.* Seek Him. Get down on your face before Him and say, "Lord, so many things are changing at my job. Am I supposed to stay here, or are You directing me elsewhere?"

Get your direction from Him. Let Him point you. Let Him become the compass for your life, so you'll know which direction to move in. He may not reveal it to the full extent that you'd like, but He'll show enough for you to take the next step, and that's all you really need. His promise to you is that His Word will be a lamp unto your feet and a light unto your path, so you won't stumble into a dark situation.

Principle #2: Stopping Comes Before Starting

There's always something you have to *stop* doing before you can *start* doing something else, and stopping it is frequently the hardest step on your journey. Sometimes God orders our steps, and sometimes He orders our stops. There's a Chinese proverb that says, "Of all the stratagems, to know when to quit is the best." You've got to know when to leave the party; you've got to know when you've been there long enough, and it's time to go.

SOMETIMES GOD ORDERS OUR *STEPS*, AND SOMETIMES HE ORDERS OUR *STOPS*.

God is often waiting for us to stop our own ways, to stop our will, so that His will can be done. He'll bring you to that place of consecration where you can make that decision. You stop trying to force your will and your way, and you say, "Lord, *Thy* will be done, *Thy* kingdom come, on earth as it is in heaven." You're giving God the go-ahead by demonstrating that your heart is in the right spot.

So when God gets ready to send you to another place, the brook will often dry up where you are, as we saw with Elijah. So if your job ends, know that God's getting ready to start something else for you. God won't leave you hanging, I promise you. Even in a situation that seems hopeless, God can create streams in the desert for you. He'll make a way out of no way because He is faithful to His Word. He'll lead you to the new position you need, or the new location, or the new relationship, or the new understanding. And to get you into them, God will put a stop to something mediocre in your life that you've been experiencing, or something that once worked for you but no longer does.

So don't be alarmed when stuff starts stopping in your life, because God's getting ready to start something better. That's His way.

When He stopped the Old Testament, He started the New. When He stopped all those ceremonial sacrifices involving the blood of bulls and goats, He started a new and eternal redemption by the blood His Son Jesus Christ! That blood was shed—once and for all—and made propitiation for our sin.

I'm here to tell you that God is taking you a step upward, to what is better, and to what is best! Things are turning around. You'd better look for God to do something in your future that's better than anything you've ever had in your past. He's not taking you backwards; He's pushing you forward to your best days.

Principle #3: Be Brutally Honest

When it's time to change your trajectory, *nothing less than brutal honesty takes you there.*

ADMIT IT AND THEN *QUIT* IT.

People don't like to admit that they aren't getting where they want to go in life. But such honesty is what it takes. So admit it; *admit it*—and then *quit it.* If you can't or won't admit that what you're doing isn't working, you'll never abandon it and move forward into something better.

If you're worn out, realize that the present course just isn't working, and finally decide to quit—it will give you more energy for something better, for your new trajectory. You'll be more *concentrated.* When you add too much water to what is concentrated, it gets thinned out. Have you ever had lemonade that was too watery or tea that was too weak, and you can't even fix it? I mean if it's too strong, you can fix it. If it's too sweet you can fix it, but if it's too weak, you can't fix it. You'll have more life potency if you're not afraid to admit that you're spreading yourself too thin—that you're just not succeeding at what you do.

But it takes brutal honesty to get to that point.

Principle #4: Tap into Your Frustrations

Instead of ignoring your frustrations, *tap into them,* because they may help you to find new direction. Dissatisfaction is a precursor to change. There are certain things in your life that will never change until you become frustrated and dissatisfied with them. God has to bring you into a position where you experience what I call "holy discontent." It's where you have to be dissatisfied with where you are.

←

DISSATISFACTION IS A PRECURSOR TO CHANGE.

→

Your frustration lets you know that you've reached a stage where you've got to move beyond it. It just isn't you anymore; you can't keep living like this. So you'll develop an intolerance in your spirit; you'll say, "I can't deal with that anymore. Don't bring me that mess anymore! I'm too old for that! I don't believe I was designed to live like this. I'm not going to spend the rest of my days like that. I could deal with it back then, but I can't deal with it now." You get frustrated, and God uses your frustration as a precursor for change. So tap into your frustrations, and they'll become for you a great sign that God is ready to shift you into another trajectory.

That's what is happening when you stop finding joy in the job that you used to be so excited and gung-ho about. It's a sign that it's time for you to go. That's what is happening when teenagers who are still living in the house with their parents start fighting with everybody and getting frustrated. It's a sign that it's time for them to go.

John Rohn said this: "Disgust and resolve are two of the great emotions that lead us to change." Tap into your frustration, and you'll see and understand how in that situation God has lifted away the grace to be able to deal with things the way you once dealt with them. When it's time for you to move on from certain things in your life or from certain people, God will strip away the grace for dealing with that problem.

Principle #5: Focus on What, Not Who

When you're changing your trajectory, focus on *what*, not *who*. It's easy to blame others for your frustrations, but don't. If something has gone wrong, don't even to try to find out whose fault it was. Don't focus on *who* made the mistake; focus on *what* we need to do to fix this. *What* happened? *What* do we do next? When you blame somebody for a problem, or make excuses based on others' mistakes (whether real or imagined), you're empowering them over your own life.

← DON'T TRY TO FIX PEOPLE, JUST FIX THE SITUATION. →

Never make the situation greater than the relationship. Never make solving the problem more important than maintaining the relationship. That's especially true in marriage and in your family. So don't try to "fix" other people; just fix the situation. It's not *who* that's your problem; it's *what*.

Principle #6: Tell Others Your Plans

You'll protect others and help yourself by observing this principle: *Tell someone else about your plans.* When you're changing your trajectory, find somebody to be a confidant. Tell them what's in your heart. Get counsel from a seasoned Christian. If you share your ideas, hopes, and plans, your friends and family will keep you accountable to them; they'll keep you on course. By telling others your plan, you give it greater life.

If you're married, absolutely never neglect to tell your wife or husband what God has placed in your heart. If you're married, you're in a partnership, and you've got to get the approval of your mate before you move forward into a big new transition. You need their support because you're going to need all the help you can get— the emotional support, spiritual support, prayer support, and every other kind of support from all those you love and who surround you in your life.

Some big decisions will need to be made as you change your trajectory. But remember this: don't decide quickly. Withhold your judgment, explore your options, consider the consequences. Take the time to slow down your thoughts and explain them to someone else. You can understand and master just about anything if you invest sufficient time studying it, reflecting on your options, and bouncing your conclusions off of someone you trust. Don't be rushed into deciding your major trajectories.

Principle #7: Increase Your Capacity

Did you know that in the parable of the talents which Jesus gives us in Matthew 25:14–30, these "talents" were not given to each individual because of favor, or because of their birth order, or even because of their righteousness? They were given on the basis of each one's *capacity*. And that parable helps us see how important it is to *increase your capacity*.

The "talent" referred to in that parable was roughly equivalent to somewhere between $10,000 and $25,000. It was bestowed on these individuals based on their ability to actually handle such an investment and to develop it. The master in the story gave one of his servants five talents, another servant two talents, and another servant one talent—"*to each according to his own ability*" (Matthew 25:15).

The two servants with greater ability were given greater amounts—and they in turn produced greater investment results. But the last servant who received the smallest amount ended up being a major disappointment.

So if you want to be trusted with more, you've got to develop your ability to handle more. Be assured that God will not entrust you with something you cannot manage. Know also that God will not entrust you with something which you cannot in turn offer to others. If you can't give something to help somebody else, God won't place it into your hands. If you can't give money, God will never entrust you with money; if you can't give praise, God will never entrust you with praise.

And here's something more: God will not entrust you with something you can't rejoice over when *others* have it and you don't. You've got to be able to celebrate the blessings in your brother's life, in your sister's life, in your friend's life. We have no business hating somebody else because of something good they've received. You've got to celebrate and say, "Thank God someone I know has been blessed with this!" Be happy for them—*honestly* happy for them. Don't be upset because someone has a finer house than you do, or a nicer car, or a better job, or whatever. You would be surprised how much people can get bent out of shape because others have something that's a little better than what they have. This tendency of our hearts is incredibly harmful, if we would just realize it!

You may not realize that the first time the word *sin* is mentioned in the Bible, it's not in reference to Adam and Eve. It appears first in Genesis 4:7, in reference to the jealousy that flared up in Cain when God accepted Abel's sacrifice but not his. Cain got upset, and God warned him, "Sin lies at the door." It was all about a jealous spirit, coveting what somebody else had. Cain had much to be thankful for, but he got so jealous over what his brother Abel had that he couldn't rejoice with him over it. He ended up becoming a murderer and an exile. So celebrate the blessings of others. If you ever want God to build something in your life, help somebody else build something. By so doing, you'll lay the groundwork for God to bring that thing back into your own life.

Principle #8: Incorporate the Old with the New

For the best wisdom in changing your trajectory, *incorporate the old with the new.* As you launch into changes in your life, don't assume that *everything* has to change. Don't throw the baby out with the bathwater.

Jesus taught us a wonderful principle in Matthew 13:52 where He said that the person instructed in the kingdom of heaven *"is like a householder who brings out of his treasure **things new and old.**"* There is *new* treasure, and there is *old* treasure—but it's all treasure. It's all valuable and worth keeping; it's of value to you and of value to the world. It would be foolish to throw away old treasure just because you've got new treasure. So we've got to learn how to creatively incorporate into our future both the old and the new.

DON'T GET OLD TOO FAST AND WISE TOO LATE.

So learn how to take old things and then create something new. Bring new value out of the old. To take something old and make something new from it—that's where genius is born. There are only three primary colors, but think of the endless array of shades and hues that can be formed from blending those three. We have only ten digits—0 through 9—but think of the infinite combinations of numbers that add up and multiply from those ten. The musical scale has seven notes—A, B, C, D, E, F, G—but think of all the countless melodies we have in this world that flow out of those seven.

It's amazing how you can take the old basics and infuse them with God-given creativity and make something brand new. That also means that when you change your trajectory, you can't throw out all your old fundamentals—don't throw out the building blocks that make you, *you*.

I get nervous if I'm involved in something and there are no middle-aged or older folks in it. I don't want just a church full of young folks. That doesn't mean I don't love young people—because I do! I love young people, and I want young people to come to church. But we also need elders in the church who have the wisdom to be able to give perspective to young people. The elders need the young folks because they've got the energy. We need the strength of their backs and the swiftness of their feet. Young folks, on the other hand, need the steadiness of our hearts and the wisdom of our minds. It really concerns me that we get old too fast and wise too late, but we can fix that if we hang around each other and realize that the two have need of each other. They are not in opposition one to another. The old can be incorporated in the new.

Principle #9: Be True to Your Own Story

To be authentic literally is to be your own author. Both of these words derive from the same Greek root (I wouldn't be Bishop Bronner if I didn't give you some etymology!). When you are true to yourself, you are living the story that God, the Author and Finisher, intended for you to live. You have to be true to your own story. God will finish everything that He has authenticated in you.

Everything that's true to your nature—if it is true to your nature—is there because God authored you. And if He said, "I'm going to make you a person of love and compassion," if that's what He's authored in you, you can try to be mean to people, you can try to be cold and indifferent and insensitive—but you've got to come back, apologize, and be loving if you're going to be true and authentic to your real self as created in Christ Jesus. God makes you go back and get it right, because He has authenticated you as a person of love and compassion. That's how He authored you, that's how He created you in His image, and that's why He redeemed you and freed you by the blood of Jesus.

Principle #10: Recognize Divine Provision and Divine Potential

The final principle for your new trajectory is *to recognize divine provision and your divine potential.* There are things that God has already built into you, and you never know it until you get into challenging situations. You don't know what you can do until you're put in a position where you've got to do it.

← ━━━━━━━━━━━━━━━━━━━━━━━━━━━━━━━━━━━━━

PROVISION COMES FOR VISION.

━━━━━━━━━━━━━━━━━━━━━━━━━━━━━━━━━━━━━ →

It's a matter of divine potential that God has placed within you: the seeds of new ideas, the seeds for new businesses and endeavors and accomplishments and creations. Perhaps you've been working hard for others, and now you're coming into a different season where you're going to be able to work hard for yourself. You've served other folks' vision; now God will entrust you with your vision. You don't have to be ashamed of your blessing that God brings into your life. Use it for His glory. Declare it for His glory: *"I am what I am by the grace of God."* (See 1 Corinthians 15:10.)

So be on the lookout for God's provision, and understand it for what it really is. Don't just start enjoying something God has currently provided without asking the question, "God, what is this for?" There is a provision, and it is for the vision. Provision comes for vision. You have incredible potential to experience a fascinating future. You've actually got more talent and more abilities than you could use up in a hundred lifetimes.

Did you know that your brain contains about 100 billion neurons, each connected to at least 20,000 other cells in a complex network in your brain? This means that all the possible combinations of thoughts and ideas you could think of would be equal to the number one followed by eight pages of zeroes. That's a number greater than all the molecules in the known universe. That's just the potential of your possibilities. It's amazing, the abilities and capacities God has placed inside us! I hope you're blown away by that, as you begin to think about who you really are. You have so much incredible potential inside you! So ask yourself, *What can I do from this day forward? What in the world can I do?* The answers are limited only by your vision, your imagination.

11

How to Be Like the Little Ant

Proverbs, as you know, is our book of wisdom, and we can glean from that wisdom every day. In Proverbs 6, beginning with verse 6, we find a familiar passage that serves as a foundation for changing our trajectory:

> Go to the ant, you sluggard! Consider her ways and be wise, which, having no captain, overseer or ruler, provides her supplies in the summer, and gathers her food in the harvest. How long will you slumber, O sluggard? When will you rise from your sleep? A little sleep, a little slumber, a little folding of the hands to sleep—so shall your poverty come on you like a prowler, and your need like an armed man. (Proverbs 6:6–11)

A Message to the Lazy

Notice that in this passage, the wise author of Proverbs is addressing himself to the "*sluggard.*" A sluggard is a lazy person; it's an *indolent* person. And one of the definitions for that word *indolent* is "avoiding pain." Isn't it interesting that lazy folks are fundamentally trying to avoid pain? Remember the little saying, "No pain, no gain."

WE WILL CHANGE ONLY WHEN THE PAIN OF REMAINING THE SAME BECOMES GREATER THAN THE PAIN OF CHANGING.

A sluggard is that lazy person sitting at home surfing the net while telling others that he's looking for a job. By such behavior he's not really benefiting himself, or anyone else either. And so this passage calls out to him, "Listen here, sluggard!" Whenever we're like that sluggard, trying to avoid pain, we fail to realize that by avoiding pain, our life will go on a steady decline. It works like this: There are a great many folks who will *never* change until the pain of *not* changing becomes too great. We will change only when the pain of remaining the same becomes greater than the pain of changing.

Notice the passage asks, "*How long will you slumber, O sluggard? When will you rise from your sleep?*" I want to give you a little bonus strategy to fight laziness. When it's time for you to get up in the morning, when the alarm clock goes off, or when you wake up and you know that this is around the time that I need to get up, don't sit there. Don't negotiate about whether it's possible to stay in bed. Just arise, because if you sit there and have the conversation, your mind will tell you, "*Go back to sleep for a few more minutes…You're tired. Just roll back over. Just a few more zzz's will do you good.*"

I don't give my mind an opportunity to have that conversation in the morning. When I wake up, I'm ready to go. I'm going to get out of there. I'm not even going to give my mind an opportunity for excusitis to start kicking in! Just get up and get out of the bed, and you shut down your mental faculties from trying to tell you, *You don't feel like it today. You're sleepy. Why don't you just push the snooze button?*

Now you may not think of yourself as being a lazy person at all, or as a person who's always trying to avoid pain. But the fact is, all of us have areas in our lives where, by applying a little more energy and diligence and self-discipline, we could make truly dramatic strides in changing the trajectory of our life. Each of us has those areas that could strongly use improvement. What are yours?

Observe and Learn

To help us out of our slackness, we're instructed here in Proverbs 6 to make the effort to *observe*—we're told to *"go"* and to *"consider"* in order to *"be wise."*

Now we're directed here specifically to observe the ant, while the key lessons derived from that observation are laid out for us in the rest of this passage. But this example of being observant toward the creation around us has a wider application. It applies especially to observing *other people*. Observe others, examine others, learn from others—and discover valuable wisdom for changing your trajectory. Observe, consider, learn—and be wise.

Some people seem to take pride in trying to discover everything for themselves. But don't be afraid to learn from others, to consult others. That's what mentoring is all about. It's gaining wisdom without having to experience the self-inflicted wounds of your own trial and error. I mean, if you see somebody else all bruised up, find out how they got that way and avoid that kind of situation yourself! You really don't have to learn the hard way by making every mistake yourself.

If, for example, you're trying to build a business, go to somebody who's had success in a similar business, and consult with them. Ask them about their greatest challenges and obstacles, their greatest rewards and successes, and the most important lessons they've learned. Observe, learn, and become wise.

Push Forward into Wisdom

When we read those words "be wise," what should that mean to us?

WISDOM TAKES THE RIGHT ACTION TODAY FOR A BETTER OUTCOME TOMORROW.

Wisdom is *applied knowledge*—it means knowledge *put into action.* There are a lot of educated folks who never really apply what they learn. I know some people who are highly educated—they've got more degrees than a thermometer—yet they don't know how to pour water out of a boot! They don't have enough sense to come in out of the rain. They've got knowledge, but it's not *applied knowledge.*

Real wisdom knows what to do, when to do it, and how to do it—and then gets right down and does it. That's wisdom. What good is it to know how to do things the right way, and yet never do them the right way? You may know quite a bit, for example, about how to take care of your health. But if you ignore those things until your body has a breakdown and your doctor has to give you some terrible news—what good has your knowledge done for you? No, wisdom looks ahead and takes the right action *today* for a better outcome *tomorrow.*

You may actually be afraid of taking action for a number of reasons. It's easy to be fearful in the face of risk and uncertainty. But consider these wise words: "The men who try to do something and fail," said Martin Lloyd Jones, "are infinitely better than those who try to do nothing and succeed."[4] And may I remind you of something Benjamin Disraeli said: "Action may not always bring happiness, but there is no happiness without action."[5] Absolutely none!

Take Initiative

While watching the ant, the keen observer recognizes that this creature is wisely busy and productive without needing to always be

4. Martin Lloyd Jones, as quoted in Roy B. Zuck, *The Speaker's Quotebook* (Grand Rapids: Kregel Publications, 2009), 182.
5. Benjamin Disraeli, *Lothair: Volume III* (London: Longmans, Green, and Co., 1870), 206.

told what to do. The ant needs *"no captain, overseer, or ruler"* (Proverbs 6:7). Here's a key lesson for us: *Take initiative.* Don't wait for somebody else to come along, take you by the hand, tell you what to do, and tell you when to get started. True leaders don't wait to be told what to do. They don't wait around until someone gives them a higher job title before they start doing a higher level of work. They see something that needs to be done, and they take initiative.

If you're on the job, and you see something that needs to be done, step forward and get it done. If it's important for others to know about it, write it up in a report and send it to management; make them aware of what you did without anybody telling you to, in order to meet a true need.

In my daddy's business, when a potential new employee was expected to come by for an interview, my daddy would scatter some litter on the front lawn. As the appointment time approached, he would look out his window and observe the person approaching the office for their interview. Most candidates saw the litter on the lawn but just kept on walking. They looked sharp and spoke well for themselves in the interview, but they didn't get the job! The person who got the job was the lady who stopped and picked up the trash. She *acted* as if she worked there before she ever really did. She was someone who took responsibility. She took the initiative. My daddy knew that the person who actually paused to pick up the trash was an *exceptional* person— and true enough, she turned out to be an exceptional employee.

Prepare for Your Next Season

We come next to the real heart of the lesson we can learn from the ant. This creature *"provides her supplies in the summer, and gathers her food in the harvest"* (Proverbs 6:8). She looks ahead and sees the future, and *prepares* for it. In the summer and at harvest-time, the ant isn't relaxing; she's thinking about winter and getting ready for it.

Here's where wisdom comes most strongly into this picture for us. God is saying, "While you're in this particular season of life, I want you to prepare for the *next* season you'll be entering." *That's wisdom.*

Don't think that the season you're in now will last forever, because it won't. God is reminding us here that the seasons of our life are going to change. *That's wisdom.*

He's reminding us to store up reserves from our abundant times in order to have it available for times of scarcity. *That's wisdom.*

In your current season, you have to start working for the season that's over the horizon. That's where most people make a big mistake. When the good times are rolling, they invite all their friends over, and they say, "Drinks on me!" They end up spending all their money on lavish living instead of using what God has given them to create a surplus for later.

So stay ahead of the curve of what's going to happen. Start doing something now in your current season that will prepare you for the uncertain days to come. And then, when you see that your season is changing, *change with it.* Change who you are and what you're doing. Adjust and modify so you don't become obsolete and mismatched for the season of life you're stepping into.

Make the Most of Each Season

There are certain things you've got to do while you can, when you're in the right season for it. It's true in the various stages of our family life, it's true in the stages of our career and at any particular job, and it's true in whatever endeavor you get involved in. There are always seasons that we go through, appropriate times for appropriate actions. By following the pattern correctly, we then bring forth our fruit in our season. You reap a harvest only by preparing for it. But if you're ignoring all that and consuming stuff in this season that was meant to be preserved for the next season as provision for the future—you're in bad shape.

Don't just sit back and enjoy the season you're in; use it to place yourself in a position of advantage for the next season approaching. Your situation now is not really about now; it's all about *later.* God sees all our future needs long before we encounter them, and He actually supplies them ahead of time. That's what you call *provision*, "the fact or state of being prepared beforehand."

GIVE WISDOM A JOB IN YOUR LIFE.

Imagine going to a car dealership in the summertime and being shown an automobile with a heater that didn't work. The dealer mentions this defect to you—but it's really warm outside, so you're thinking, *who needs a heater?* Then when winter hits, as it always does, are you going to be surprised to find yourself freezing every time you drive to work or to the store? That would be stupid. But unfortunately, that's what we do in many areas of life. There are many folks who would be in deep trouble if their salary was cut off even just for a month. They are not prepared.

Faith and Wisdom

Things might be good for you now, but they simply aren't always going to be that way. So God says, "Prepare yourself in good times for bad times." This was the wisdom God gave to Joseph in the Old Testament. God showed him that Egypt's seven years of prosperity and plentiful harvest were going to be followed by seven lean years. And because Joseph was *"a discerning and wise man"* and *"a man in whom is the Spirit of God"* (Genesis 41:33, 38), he launched and oversaw a vast program of storing up crop reserves, allowing that nation and its neighbors to survive a long and severe famine. *That's wisdom.*

So I don't understand how some people can say that preparing yourself for turbulent times in the future is somehow against faith. Actually, faith and wisdom go hand in hand.

Whenever you face transition and change, you must employ wisdom. Give wisdom a job in your life—the job God intended for it. In Proverbs 4:7, God says this: *"Wisdom is the principal thing; therefore get wisdom."* Notice that this verse doesn't say *faith* is the principal thing, and it doesn't say *money* is the principal thing. Here's why: if you've got wisdom, wisdom will let you know what it really means to have faith in God. Wisdom will let you know how and when to make money, to save money, and to use money. Remember, faith is not a substitute for wisdom. God will give you the wisdom to be able to know how to live by faith.

Proverbs also tells us this about both foolishness and wisdom: *"The simple believes every word, but the prudent considers well his steps. A wise man fears and departs from evil, but a fool rages and is self-confident"* (Proverbs 14:15–16). Isn't that amazing? Our faith in God and in His Word should lead us to learn and hold on tight to these principles of wisdom.

Strength for a New Season

Recall the scene in 1 Kings 19, after the prophet Elijah had seen God's victory and judgment on Mount Carmel against the prophets of Baal. Immediately afterward, Elijah found himself running away from the wicked Queen Jezebel, afraid for his life. He went a day's journey into the wilderness, then plopped himself on the ground under a tree, exhausted and ready for his life to end.

Then we read about God's gracious care for him:

Suddenly an angel touched him, and said to him, "Arise and eat." Then he looked, and there by his head was a cake baked on coals, and a jar of water. So he ate and drank, and lay down again.

(1 Kings 19:5–6)

Another special provision comes next:

And the angel of the LORD *came back the second time, and touched him, and said, "Arise and eat, because the journey is too great for you." So he arose, and ate and drank; and he went in the strength of that food forty days and forty nights as far as Horeb, the mountain of God.*

(verses 7–8)

The first time Elijah was given food by the angel, it was to restore him for the season he was in. But the second time this happened, it was for the season just ahead. The angel of God was telling him, "You need to eat more now because of *where you're going*. Feed yourself for the next season of your life." And because of that replenishment of strength, Elijah was able to journey onward for forty days. So will God give us strength for the seasons ahead.

Rise from Your Slumber—and Prepare!

Let's return once more to that little ant in Proverbs 6. Notice again the concluding words in this life-lesson that we're given here:

> *How long will you slumber, O sluggard? When will you rise from your sleep? A little sleep, a little slumber, a little folding of the hands to sleep—so shall your poverty come on you like a prowler, and your need like an armed man.*   (Proverbs 6:9–11)

Here's the message for us in that: *Wake up and be aware!*

When you read the Bible, don't just read it like a history book. Keep asking the question, "Lord, what are *You* saying to *me* through this Word?" Be awake and be aware!

From the ant in Proverbs 6, we could summarize the lesson we've learned in these words: *Be aware...and prepare!* Let your preparation extend to all of life. Remember that as things change around you, you've got to be prepared on so many different levels. Let me quickly remind you of just a few of them:

First, *personal preparation.* This includes understanding the impact of our character, temperament, and personality on our future effectiveness, especially in how we influence others. Remember, leadership is not really about leading *others*; it's about leading *yourself* in a way that *inspires* others to follow. *Prepare yourself first.*

Second, *professional preparation.* This involves staying current in your area of competence. If you're going to do something, do it well.

And if you're getting ready to launch a business, remember that you need *competence*, you need *content*, and you need *capital*. That's all part of your professional preparation.

Third, *relational preparation*. This includes being aware of your "chemistry" with others and your ability to get along with all types of people. If God's going to bless you and take you to a higher level, you've got to be able to work with people who don't think how you think or look like you look. You've got to be able to get along with all kinds of people, because God very often will provide something you need in somebody that you don't like. In your relational preparation, learn to remove and overcome the obstacles that would keep you from knowing and benefitting from others.

Fourth, *family preparation*. Ensure that the people you love most are ready for whatever they'll face in connection with your new trajectory, because when your life changes, your whole family has to adapt in some way to what's going on in your life. For example, the next step in your career might involve a move to another city. For your children, that would mean being uprooted from the friends they've made and the school and the teachers they've grown accustomed to. So prepare your family for whatever is happening in your life.

Fifth, *financial preparation*. This involves arranging your income and your expenses for your future. Remember that whenever you spend money and go in debt to do it, you're robbing from your future to enhance your present. But whenever you invest, you're borrowing from your present to enhance your future. You have to be financially prepared.

And finally, *educational preparation*. This may include taking classes, earning a degree, reading, joining professional associations, and attending seminars. It also certainly includes faithfully attending church, which is all about preparing and equipping us by the Word of God for life so that we can move forward in new ways. Through these preparatory steps, you'll be stretched in your faith, your thinking, and your perspective for a fuller understanding of the new trajectory God is bringing to you.

12

How to Sweat,
but Not Too Much

I know you've heard the saying "Don't sweat the small stuff," but change is not small stuff. We're supposed to sweat a bit over change. A normal body, when it moves from rest to activity, is prone to sweat because sweating is a natural part of the process of helping the body to rid itself of toxins. Impurities leave your system when you sweat. So why wouldn't you want to sweat, especially when big stuff happens? You want your body to notice when things are changing; what you *don't* want, however, is for the changes to start ruling your body through the painful grip of stress.

Every life change creates stress whether it is losing a job and having to search for another, or divorcing and adjusting to singleness again, or what have you. A major change immediately thrusts your life into transition. Remember change and transition are not the same. Change is the event of something that happened while transition is the psychological, emotional, financial, relational and spiritual processing of change. It is during transition that we experience our greatest levels of stress. Our greatest anxiety doesn't come from thinking about our future, but from our trying to control it. You've got to come to grips with the fact that you cannot control everything that happens in your future. No one can. So do your best and trust God for the rest! Never quit something with long term potential just because you can't deal with the stress of the moment.

We encounter the stress of a transition when the rate of change is too rapid or the sheer amount of change is too overwhelming, and there's so much to learn so quickly. We say, "I'll never understand this! It's just too much!" We're all creatures of habit to some extent, and when our routines are upset, it's stressful. Stress, of course, can also come from too little change. If you're in a situation where something needs to change, yet nothing's changing, you can get stressed out. You'll hear yourself saying, "I'm tired of dealing with this same old mess."

When an elementary student is promoted to middle school, she is stressed trying to adjust to a new environment. The same kind of stress is experienced when that student transitions to high school, and then again when she graduates and matriculates in college. I will never forget the stress I felt as a senior in high school. A myriad of questions bombarded my mind. I wondered:

- Will my SAT scores be high enough to win a scholarship?
- Which college should I attend?
- Should I remain at home or go out of town?
- What should be my major?
- Will college work be significantly harder than high school?
- Will I be able to successfully handle the new level of independence and personal responsibility?
- Will it be easy to make new friends?

And the list went on.

During childbirth a pregnant woman enters the final stage of active labor, conveniently referred to as "transition" or "transitional labor." As a part of labor and delivery, transition is the most difficult phase of labor for most women because it's the most painfully intense. But there is some good news about transition—it is the shortest phase of labor! The mother generally experiences her greatest stress during this period. As the pain of contractions intensify, she has a natural tendency to tense her body in response.

SEVEN IN TEN AMERICANS EXPERIENCE SYMPTOMS OF STRESS.

Likewise, as you are changing your trajectory, you will experience stress that can make you tense and panicky. But it dawned on me one day that stress is normal to life, just as problems are normal to life. I discovered that I didn't have to allow stress to paralyze me. I learned to feel the stress and keep moving with the right perspective. I realized that problems are situations that can be solved, but a fact of life is that which must be accepted. The key is to never construe a problem as a fact of life.

Bad Stress Versus Good Stress

The American Psychological Association reports that approximately seven in ten Americans experience physical or non-physical symptoms of stress.[6] That's a lot of people! Chances are great that you're stressed out right now—and that can lead to sleepless nights and irritable days. Stress can make some people tired, sad, and even paralyzed from moving forward. Stress can result in poor eating habits. Stress can age you prematurely. Stress can even kill. Thus, transition is a time that you must take extra caution in taking care of yourself. If you don't know how to effectively harness the energy of stress, it can overwhelm you. Bad stress can cause you to imagine the worst-case scenario happening and spark a panic attack.

Not all stress, however, is bad. Good stress can bring out the best in you. Good stress stretches but doesn't overwhelm. Some people do

6. See "Impact of Stress," American Psychological Association, www.apa.org/news/press/releases/stress/2012/impact.aspx (accessed 22 April 2013).

their best work under last minute pressure! Good stress drives you to search for answers. It connects you with others. It motivates you to effectively utilize your resources. Good stress even helps you to maximize the moment and focus so you can creatively apply your skills.

I find that people are most receptive to God when they're under the stress of transition. They're looking for Him because they need help. That's good, because whenever you're in a season of transition and change, you need divine guidance and godly wisdom.

What Causes Stress?

Have you ever stopped simply to think about what actually causes you to stress out? One of the greatest internal causes of stress is living out of sync with who you are! When what you feel on the inside does not match what you experience on the outside, the result is often stress and frustration. Knowing yourself frees you from living inconsistently and enables you to live within your values. Additionally, it strengthens your resolve to withstand pressure to conform to the expectations of others.

Another huge cause of stress, especially for nice, friendly, volunteer-oriented people, is saying "Yes" when you should say "No." And when you think about it, the main reason a person has a hard time saying "No" is generally because he/she is out of sync with himself/herself. Having an understanding of who you are helps to give you clarity of what you should be doing. Knowing who you are includes understanding your life's mission. A powerful key to inner peace is living according to your inner core, as I mentioned in chapter 9.

A third cause of stress is trying to control things you cannot control. You can only—theoretically—control what you yourself do. You cannot control other people and the whimsical choices they make. You cannot control many external circumstances. I wish I could control traffic. I wish I could control the weather. I wish I could control people's negative opinions and actions. I am liberated by realizing that I cannot control people and oftentimes, the circumstances they create. I can only control my attitude and my response to what happens to me. Now while I cannot control people, I am grateful that I can often influence how they think and behave.

ROUTINES BEGIN AS DRUDGERY BUT END UP AS DELIGHT.

A fourth cause of stress is to have irresponsible or uncommitted people as a member of your team. It is unfair that no matter how large a family is, the major bulk of responsibility usually finds itself on the shoulders of one person. If you are working on a project in school or at work and you are working really hard to make it as good as it can be, you will inevitably discover slackers whose contribution is minimal at best! This can be a huge sore spot and cause of stress. Although this is frustrating to me, I simply remember the saying, "To whom much is given, much is also required."

Relieving Stress

Perhaps one of the greatest stress relievers is developing competent, reliable people around you. Before you attempt to build a business, a school, a ministry, or a project, carefully and prayerfully select the team that will assist you. The greatest source of stress is wrong personnel on the team. The greatest source of stress relief is the right personnel on the team.

As you move through transition as a part of changing your trajectory in life, spend some quality time reflecting, evaluating and making adjustments. Ask yourself, "What are my greatest causes of stress?" Then make a list of them. Here are a few common ones to jumpstart your thinking:

+ Money

+ Relationship issues

+ Unrealistic expectations of others

+ Health problems

+ Deadlines for assignments

Now I want you to think about some healthy ways to diffuse your stress. The things that counter stress are *simple*; but not everything that is *simple* is *easy*! Here are a few simple suggestions:

1. Depend on your relationship with God—commune with Him. Pray each day. Read your Bible. Meditate.

2. Develop as many routines in your life as possible—the less you have to think about, the less stress you feel over them. Routines begin as drudgery but end up as delight.

3. Start whatever you do in plenty of time. Discipline is about valuing what you want *most* over what you want *now*! Discipline involves delaying personal gratification.

4. Anticipate negative things happening and think of alternative ways of dealing with them. Be proactive. Psychologists have found that people who dream about negative events (i.e. getting fired from work) actually respond better to them when they happen in reality than those who never saw it coming.

5. Join a support group. Associating with people who have a similar situation to yours can help you find strength. Having someone who can relate to how you are feeling is invaluable. Having someone to talk to is a gift. Having someone to listen to you is a treasure. You find understanding and support when you integrate into society as opposed to isolating from society.

6. Find healthy ways to de-stress—what relaxes you? Here are some simple ideas that may prove helpful to you:

+ A walk in the park/nature

- Owning and caring for a pet
- Working out at the gym/exercising
- Having sex (in the context of marriage)
- Taking a warm bath
- Listening to soothing music
- Getting a massage/aromatherapy
- Reading
- Journaling
- Taking a vacation
- Playing sports
- Playing games and having fun with your children.

Think further about various ways that you personally unwind best. And remember, life is a collection of moments. So learn to have joy in the journey!

13

How to Deal with Failure

Y ou knew it was coming. You've been reading all my insight on how to *succeed*, and you're thinking, *but what if I fail?* Let me offer you two big but simple truths about failure.

First, *failures are normal and inevitable.* Show me a person who has never failed, and I'll show you a person who's never done anything. Failure is a normal part of life.

Second, *failure is the womb of success.* It's the thing that births something new out of you. All true success is born out of failure.

← FAILURE IS THE WOMB OF SUCCESS. →

Let me reiterate that second point: *Failure always precedes success.* Almost never does a person attempt to do something for the first time, and immediately do it better than they'll ever do it again. Remember, the only time you start out on top is when you're digging a hole. But you don't *build* something by starting at the top. You'll never start off as good at something as you can later become. No matter how naturally talented you are, your natural talent can always be developed to a higher level by practice.

GOALS ARE A DEADLINE FOR YOUR DREAMS.

One of the greatest things that hinders people from pursuing their dreams is the fear of failure. But since failures are not only inevitable but also good and necessary for our ongoing success, there's no particular reason to be so afraid of them. The world forgives us when we make mistakes, but the world forgets folks who did nothing. Henry Link says, "While one person hesitates because he feels inferior, the other person is busy making mistakes and becoming superior."[7]

In this chapter I want to quickly look at some of the reasons people fail. Thinking about them might help you safeguard yourself from making these errors—or at least to more quickly and clearly recognize the fact that you've already made them. Usually, when we experience failure, part of God's purpose behind that situation is to help us learn some specific lessons and perspectives in one or more of these areas.

Unrealistic Goals

People often fail because they have unrealistic goals. Maybe you've decided you can lose seventy pounds in two weeks. I'm sorry, that's not realistic. It's not an unworthy goal, but it is an unattainable goal, in all practicality.

You might see an advertisement stating that you can join some sales program and start making $20,000 a month, just like so-and-so has done. You see yourself signing on and having a goal to reach that $20,000 figure the first month, or the second at the latest. What they don't tell you in

---

7. Henry C. Link, as quoted in M.P. Singh, *Quote Unquote* (New Delhi: Lotus Press, 2006), 211.

the advertisement is that it actually took years for so-and-so to reach that level, or that he started out with several hundred contacts to call on while you only know about six people. You've set an unrealistic goal.

Goals are a deadline for your dreams, and they are a great tool for productivity. But your goal must be attainable, or it will end up being counterproductive. Too many people want to fly before they learn to crawl.

Misappropriated Resources

Another reason for failure is misappropriated resources—using your money or your time or other resources for the wrong things or in the wrong place.

If you spend your time or your money wrongly, so that these resources aren't really serving your vision and your purpose, then you've misappropriated them. The same is true about the work or service provided by people who are helping you; if they're working in the wrong area, that's a misappropriated resource.

We have all misappropriated resources, haven't we? I'm sure you wish you had all that money returned to you that you've misappropriated over the years—all the money you threw away on stuff that didn't matter. And the same is true for the time you've wasted. What do you do when nobody is looking? You are really only as committed as you are in the uninspected or ungoverned areas of your life. It's what you do in your leisure time—especially for men—that really makes you or breaks you. If you're spending the majority of your leisure time gaming, then you might face failure in the future from misappropriating your time. You are not made by what you do at work, but what you do when you are not at work.

Changing Conditions and Circumstances

Changing conditions and circumstances are another reason for failure. Some people fail just because the market changed, or business conditions suddenly deteriorated. People get upside down on their house payments because of the turmoil in the housing market and the mortgage industry. In today's world of constantly increasing changes, this is a frequent reason for people's failures.

Lack of Skill and Preparation

People also fail because of lack of skill. They don't have sufficient expertise for what they're attempting to do, and that sets them up for failure. You can have great desires and an exciting goal. But you need more than that to succeed; you must also have some skill.

PRACTICE DOESN'T MAKE PERFECT, BUT IT DOES MAKE BETTER.

You can't just want to be a baker; you've got to know how to read a recipe and work some dough. You can't just have this dream to become a ballerina; you have to learn balance and poise. You're not going to be first-string on the football team if you don't have the aptitude for it. You can be a legend in your own mind, but that doesn't succeed in the real world. No, you've got to have skill. And even if you're not the world's best, if you practice, you will become better. Practice doesn't make perfect, but it does make better.

There's a difference between planning something and preparing something. You can plan the dinner, but when you prepare for dinner, you've got to actually get the chicken out. You've got to snap the beans. You've got to mash the potatoes. It's a process. Preparation is getting all the necessary ingredients and resources together. If you just plan and plan and plan, that's like taking a gun and aiming it here, then there, then over there. But if you are going to execute a plan, you need to learn how to pull the trigger! If you are going to accomplish something, you can't just plan. You have to prepare. Poor preparation is, in essence, the reason for every failure.

Inadequate or Inaccurate Information

Another reason for failure is inadequate or inaccurate information. You may have made a decision but didn't have sufficient information to make a *good* decision.

Have you ever made a bad choice on something because you were misinformed, or you just weren't knowledgeable enough about the whole thing? Sometimes other people pull the wool over your eyes and prevent you from knowing what you need to know. You can spend too much money on something because you didn't know the product's real value, didn't read the fine print, and somebody was talking real fast trying to sell it to you.

It's important, when you're gathering facts, to be balanced and use both positive and negative thinking. Positive thinking allows us to see the merits, benefits, and advantages of our ideas or plans. Positive thinking always looks at what's right with the idea, and why it will succeed. Negative thinking, on the other hand, allows one to see the risks, dangers, errors, pitfalls, disadvantages, or difficulties of pursuing a certain line of action. Negative thinking actually helps us to correct our ideas, make them realistic, and make better plans in the long run. When I look at something that I am getting ready to do, I play the devil's advocate. I ask myself, *why will this plan fail?* That questions sends me on the search more for information and forces me to rebuild my plan so it's airtight from things that would keep it from working. That way, you prepare yourself for success.

Wrong Assumptions

People also fail because of wrong assumptions. You assumed that because you opened up a business, people were going to rush through your doors to get what you have for sale because you're carrying superior products. But it was a wrong assumption.

START PUTTING YOUR IDEAS ON A JOURNEY.

Now, let me clarify myself. You ought to have positive expectations. When you get ready to go into business, or open a school, or create a piece of art—whatever you do—you ought to expect it to do well, and expect to have that recognized by others. However, sometimes we make wrong assumptions that are poorly grounded in reality. We so often guesstimate about how much work something will involve, or how much time it will take, or how much money it will cost, and our guess is way off the mark. We had a plan, yet the assumptions we built into our plan just were not realistic.

Don't assume that you'll be able to get something off the ground right away. You might have a great idea, but don't quit your day job in pursuit of that great idea. Don't wait until the world is going to pay you full time to do what you love; do it on the side. Keep your day job, and do what you love on the side until it's able to fully support you. Start putting your ideas on a journey, start working on them on a volunteer basis while nobody's willing to pay you a dime for it. Assume it won't make money for years. You know, my first few years of ministry, I didn't accept a dime of income from what I was doing. I gave it all back to the ministry because I wasn't doing it for the money. I'm still not doing it for the money, and I don't ever assume that ministry will make me the big bucks. You have to have the right assumptions.

How to Fail Well

Finally, I want to share some helpful guidelines for how to fail well.

First of all, *don't overreact when you fail.* Crying and moping around for days makes you look weak and insecure. Remember, everybody fails; failure is normal; failure is inevitable. Remember too that you learn your greatest lessons from your failures, not from your successes. You've been down that road, and you found out the bridge was out, and it taught you to take a different path and a better one. You trusted people, and they took advantage of you, but next time you'll be more careful about who you trust.

Second, *don't pretend everything's okay*. I don't like failure; I don't think anybody likes to fail. But don't hide your disappointment by pretending the failure didn't happen. That makes you look disconnected and out of touch.

AN EXCUSE IS A LIE DISGUISED AS A REASON.

Third, *take responsibility; don't blame others*. Remember that when you blame someone in your life, you empower them. If you say, "It was their fault," you're declaring that they've got more control over your destiny than you do. So don't blame. Take responsibility. When you fail, ask questions like: Have I contributed in any way to this failure by a lack of attention to detail? Have I contributed to my failure by a lack of preparation? Did I contribute to my failure because of a broken focus? Did I contribute to my failure because of naiveté? What does God want me to learn from this failure?

People respect responsible leaders who ask questions like these. God did not have respect for Adam when he blamed his sin on Eve, because he refused to accept responsibility. *Denial* means refusing to accept responsibility, and that's what Adam did. He just made up an excuse and blamed the sin on his wife.

Eliminate the excuses that keep you where you are. An excuse is a lie disguised as a reason. That's a Dale Bronner original! I just gave that to you out of my stash. "Well done!" is always better than "well said!" So instead of trying to explain your failure, just get up off the floor and try something different. Go ahead and do it because if you look for an excuse you will always find one.

And finally, if you really want to fail well, *let yourself admit, "I was wrong."* I don't know why, but I believe it's statistically factual that it is more difficult for men to say those words than it is for women. I think it's the way men's mouths are made. I think it's a physiological deformity that it takes a whole lot of effort for me to even say, "I was wrong." But seriously, if you recognize the mistakes you made that led to your failure, be honest about them.

And learn from those mistakes; don't persist in them. One of the worst things is to be persistently, stubbornly wrong. Now there's certainly a place for the philosophy of "if at first you don't succeed, try, try again." But you probably need to change a few things in your further attempts. If you're obviously headed down the wrong road—a road that leads nowhere, a track that's a dead end—the best thing you can do is switch tracks.

The place for persistence is when you know where you're going, and you know you're on the right track. That's when persistence is the best thing in the world. If the path you're on is indeed creating the trajectory you desire, then *persist*; if not, begin creating and following a new path. Get before God to confirm that it's the right one...and then persist. Persist through all the day-today difficulties. Never quit something with great long-term potential just because you dislike the stress of the moment. Learn from that stress and your responses to stress, learn from any momentary failures it might produce...and then move forward persistently toward the goal and the vision God has given you.

14

How to Pray

You'll never advance to a place in life where you don't need God. God never designed us to "grow up" and become independent of Him; we will always have reason to lift up our life to Him in prayer. You will sincerely seek God's help when you stop and realize how desperately you need it because of the rampant change all around you. There's really only one kind of prayer God answers—and that is a desperate prayer. The degree that we're really desperate for God will determine the measure into which He will show up in our lives to do the miraculous and the impossible.

PEOPLE WHO CAN'T FIND THE TIME TO PRAY WILL ALWAYS FIND TIME TO WORRY.

When you really start to see what God has for you, you'll find yourself praying for it. Can you believe that God can let you utter a prayer, and it touches heaven, and then the power and the grace of God will come down to earth—all because you prayed? Let me tell you one of the things that grieves the heart of God. We get offended over unanswered prayers, but God gets offended over unoffered prayers—when we don't even take the time to pray. Prayer is about a quiet time, where you settle down and stop the busyness of life that can get you away from God.

It's interesting to me that the people who can't find the time to pray will always find time to worry. But you'll discover that if you pray more, you have less to worry about. And when you do pray, when you're sincerely asking God to help you—let me tell you, God will bestow His favor on you!

I mean, when the alarm goes off and your eyes open up, you ought to think a God-thought, "Lord, thank You for grace for another day. Thank You that this day that Your mercies are made new to me. Thank You!" Something ought to bubble up first thing in the morning. You shouldn't start running down this list of what all you need to do today and the fact that you're running late. You ought to say, "Lord, I thank You!" Make it a part of your daily journey.

The Devil's Strategy

It is the strategy of the devil to get us so busy on our feet that we don't have time to get on our knees. Have you ever just taken the time to just get quiet? Have you ever woken up in middle of the night and began to hear all of the weird sounds that are happening in your house? The floor creaking, things in the ceiling shifting. You know temperature changes cause things to move. In the nighttime, if you could hear it, if your room is near the kitchen, you'll actually hear the motor on your refrigerator or freezer. Let me tell you this: the floor creaks during the daytime, as does the ceiling, and the refrigerator's motor goes on and off, but we don't hear it because we're too busy. It's not until you get quiet in the night that you can hear stuff that goes totally unnoticed in the noise and the busyness of the day.

In the same way, there is so much that we miss spiritually because we are too oversaturated with stimuli to even notice. Coming events often send soft, subtle signals, but we are seldom quiet enough to hear them. When was the last time that you sat quietly and just listened to what was going on in the world around you? When was the last time that you were in "receive" mode instead of "transmit" mode? When was the last time that you just sat there not trying to figure something out, not trying to exercise, not doing anything on the computer, not on your cell phone, not eating a snack, not even listening to music? A time where you don't think; you just look, you see, you feel, you smell, you listen. When was the last time that you just sat and had a time of quiet reflection and a pensive mood before God? What makes you think that you always just have to be doing something? Remember that we are human *beings* not human *doings*.

WE ARE HUMAN *BEINGS* NOT HUMAN *DOINGS*.

Some people get their greatest insights when they're in the shower. You know why? Because the shower is a routine activity for us. It puts your mind on autopilot because when you shower you're washing the same body you've washed your whole life, so you don't even have to think about it. Then the water creates "white noise" that actually allows your soul to simply reflect, and some of the greatest thoughts come to people while they're taking their shower.

Prayer has the same effect, although even greater. If for nothing else, we need prayer to maintain patience and to be able to hold onto our peace. There are three keys to changing your trajectory: 1) prayer, 2) prayer, and 3) prayer. Prayer is the lifeline of the believer. Prayer will get us in. Prayer will get us through. Prayer will get us out. If you're out of a job, prayer can get you in. If you're in a bad situation, prayer can get you out of it. If you're in a "pickle" and you don't know whether you can make it through this thing, prayer can get you through it. If you're in trouble, if you're in hot water, prayer can help you. I'm just telling you, we've got to learn to pray.

Prayer is a powerful thing. No wonder Charles Spurgeon said, "I would rather teach one man to pray than ten men to preach." You know why? The devil is never intimidated by prayer-less preaching or prayer-less teaching. He is not intimidated by prayer-less witnessing to somebody because your witness does not have power unless you pray. He's not intimidated by prayer-less churches.

You can tell what the devil is really against by what he fights. And he must really be against prayer, because he fights it tooth and nail. The three top ways that Satan fights prayer, and the first one is straight-up sleepiness. Anybody ever been there? It's time to pray, and it's like your eyelids get so heavy that you just can't focus! If that happens, change up your sequence. If the devil is trying to put you to sleep on your knees, stand up! You won't fall asleep standing up. If you do get tempted to fall asleep standing up, walk around instead of staying in one place! Pray on the move! You have to have tactics to counter him. When you know his tactics, you know how to plan your counterattack.

YOU CAN TELL WHAT THE DEVIL IS REALLY AGAINST BY WHAT HE FIGHTS.

Here's the second tactic that he uses: wandering thoughts. Have you ever sat down to pray, and then your mind just starts figuring out what in the world you're gonna eat, and what's coming on TV, and what all you have to do, and you're not even there with God. It's a satanic distraction. If your mind is wandering, put on worship music. Lift up your hands while you pray. Have an actual list of things that you want to make sure that you include during your time of prayer. You have to have counterattacks for the devil.

The third tactic that he uses is interruptions. Have you ever been on your knees, or in your bathroom praying, and then somebody starts calling your name, "Mama!"? The moment you get in prayer, somebody's gonna call your name, the doorbell rings, your cell phone goes off. You ever notice that? Just interruptions. It didn't even happen until you started praying.

So Satan uses sleepiness and wandering thoughts and interruptions. You have to be aware of his tactics, and you have to choose a time of day that works best for you where you'll experience the least distractions and where you'll be most focused. First thing in the morning might sound like a good time for prayer, but it's actually a horrible time for night owls. They can barely find their toothbrush in the morning, let alone focus on prayer! Or some folks work all night, and they're just getting home in the morning. They need to go to bed. They're not going to be very effective. They need to wait until they have an alert time. Find a time where you're alert, and resolve to pray at that time, even for a short while, every day. If you've got a problem even being able to be disciplined in praying by yourself, then find somebody to pray with. Sharing encouragement is always a motivation. Get a prayer partner, an accountability person for your prayer life.

God feels the joy and the excitement and the sorrow and the pain that we have at that moment when we pray. He knows that there are times when we don't even know what to say—and that's okay! He's God. We're permitted to just rest in Him and do what I call "praying without words." Have you ever seen true friends that can be in each other's company and don't even have to talk? You ever seen people that have been married for a long time? You see them out in a restaurant, two old folks, and they don't even open their mouths. The whole time, they're in total silence! You know when you've been together a long time, you know what the other one's thinking anyway. You have heard all of their stories—you know what they're feeling before they say it. You don't need words. When you know each other that well, you can be with each other and your presence communicates. Sometimes our prayer is simply our worshipful presence communicating with God.

Prayer is as important as your breathing. It's impossible to be an authentic Christian and not be a praying Christian. Do you know that with any successful relationship, there needs to be communication? Can you imagine having somebody that you call your real friend, but they never call you, never visit you, never want to talk to you? The friendship and the relationship would deteriorate very rapidly if there was no communication. Please understand this; prayer is not talking to the wall. When we pray we are talking to *somebody*. When we pray we are communicating with a real Person, a real God, a real Holy Spirit. We're talking to somebody who hears us and who understands us.

Three Suggestions for Prayer

Here are a few suggestions that I want you to think about as you start your prayer life. 1. Choose a daily time to meet with God. If you don't set an appointment, you won't find the time. Establish a regimen of prayer. Set a time for it. Fix the time firmly in your mind. Don't just pray when you feel like it. Let me say this to you; it is better for you to carve out quiet time that is short but regular than to have lengthy but random times with God. Have an appointment with God and keep it. If your primary prayer time is not when you first get up in the morning, remember, nonetheless, to contact God the second you open your eyes and dedicate your day to Him.

2. Set a specific amount of time for your daily appointment with God. Make it small at first and then gradually increase it. At times it may increase if you've got some other stuff going, or sometimes certain emergencies that might come in your life might reduce that time, but if you make your prayers short, also make sure to make them frequent.

3. Choose a regular location where you can meet with God. Prayer has to happen somewhere. You need to have a prayer chamber, a place where you pray—undistracted. It's fine to pray while you're driving in the car and riding on the bus, but you need an undistracted time of prayer. It may be in your office, in your bedroom, or in a garden, some-place where interruptions will be at a minimum.

I also want to encourage you to use a model for prayer for those times that you don't have a direct Spirit-led prayer initiative. I'm going to give you three different models—use whichever one you like the best, or use all three! Just as long as you're praying.

The "Lord's Prayer"

Pray through the Lord's Prayer. (See Matthew 6:9–15 KJV.)

"Our Father, which art in Heaven": picture Calvary and thank God that you can call Him Father by the virtue of the blood of Jesus. *"Hallowed be Thy name"*: hallow, or praise, the names of God, because by so doing you'll make a faith declaration. Here are few examples of God's name: *Jehovah Jireh*, the Lord my Provider; *El Shaddai*, the All-Sufficient One; *Jehovah Shalom*, the Lord my Peace; *Jehovah Rohi*, the Lord my Shepherd. *"The name of the LORD is a strong tower; the righteous run to it, and they are safe"* (Proverbs 18:10)!

"Thy Kingdom come, Thy will be done": ask the Lord for His kingdom to reign in every sphere of your life, in your spiritual life, in your family, in your church, in your pastor, in your job, in your state, in your nation, in the whole earth.

> ### "WE HAVE TO PRAY WITH OUR EYES ON GOD NOT ON THE DIFFICULTIES."

Then you move into your petitions, *"Give us this day our daily bread"*: Christ said to let our requests be made known unto God. We can come boldly to His throne and let our requests be made known to Him—not just what's going on but what you want to go on. Oswald Chambers said, "We have to pray with our eyes on God not on the difficulties." Then when you pray, give God time to respond in your spirit. Give Him time to impart His wisdom into your heart as to what you should do. Realize that time spent with God is never wasted. Be specific, even tenacious, and make your supplications known unto God.

"And forgive us our debts as we forgive our debtors": That's where you ask God to forgive you and then you release others that you're holding stuff against. Ask the Holy Spirit to even show you people that you might have an issue with that you haven't realized yet, and you set your will to forgive those who've sinned against you.

Then, *"And lead us not into temptation but deliver us from evil"*: That means you put on the whole armor of God. Put on the whole armor of God: your loins girded about with truth, putting on the breastplate of righteousness, your feet shod with the preparation of the gospel of peace, the shield of faith, the helmet of salvation, the sword of the Spirit, and then praying with all prayer in the Spirit and with supplication. You pray a hedge of protection around yourself and your loved ones. (See Ephesians 6:13–18).

And finally, *"For Thine is the Kingdom, the power, and the glory"*: This is where you make your faith declaration. You close your prayer in praise. You open it hallowing and praising His name, and you close it with praise. You thank Him for what He's *already* done and you thank Him for what He's *about* to do.

ACTS

There's another model of prayer that you could use, called the "ACTS" model because of its use of an acronym. The "A" is *adoration*. You praise God for who He is. Adore Him; praise Him for who He is. The "C" is *confession*. You tell Him everything that you've done wrong and you ask for His forgiveness. You can't wait and confess once a year—you've done too much to wait that long! You've got to confess your sin daily. You forget all the mess you've done if you don't confess daily. Confession is like a bar of soap for bathing daily. Can you imagine how filthy and grimy you'd be if you didn't wash for a year—or even a week? Similarly, you have to confess daily.

"T" is *thanksgiving*; thanking God for prayers answered and for helping us in our daily lives. Thanking Him for His goodness, mercy, favor, grace, healing, and anointing in your life. Thanking Him for your family…in everything give thanks, like it says in the book of James.

Then, finally, the "S" is *supplication*. Finish your prayer by asking God for your daily meal, for healing, for blessing. Notice that the structure of the ACTS prayer keeps you from focusing on yourself and forces you to focus on God. You know something's wrong with your prayer when it's full of supplication and nothing else—then it's all me, me, me. But when first you express your adoration, then your confession, then your thanksgiving, and all that comes before telling God what *you* want, then your heart is in the right place.

The Tabernacle Prayer

In the Tabernacle Prayer, every piece of furniture that was in the Old Testament Tabernacle becomes something that we pray for. You walk through the tabernacle in your mind, and you pray. Use the various pieces of furniture as a reference point in prayer. Each piece is strategically placed on purpose and can be used to give you an outline for personal prayer. There are three principal sections of the tabernacle—the outer court, the inner court, and the Holy of holies. Each section represents a process of how to approach the holy throne of God in prayer.

YOU LEARN HOW TO PRAY BY PRAYING.

The brazen altar in the outer court is the place where we thank God for the shed blood of Jesus that saves us. We are saved by the blood of Jesus Christ. Then the brazen laver is where we are washed by the water of the Word. The blood is messy, but it atones for our sin; yet, you need the water to wash the scarring away. Then you come into the inner court, and in that you'll find the golden lamp stand with seven branches. These seven branches are the seven spirits of God that are talked about in Isaiah 11: the Spirit of the Lord, the spirit of wisdom, the spirit of understanding, the spirit of counsel, the spirit of knowledge, the spirit of might, and the spirit of the fear of the Lord. After you go through all that, and you want to thank God.

In the inner court, you also find the table of showbread. This is where you have communion with God, brought about by the body and blood of Christ. As He said, "Except you eat My flesh and drink My blood you have no part of Me." (See John 6:53.) It's where we come into fellowship with Him, have communion with Him, and talk with Him. Also in that court is the altar of incense. This is where, after you've done all of the praying that you know how to do in your conscious mind, you allow the Holy Spirit and other tongues to rise up before God and pray unto God things that you don't even know you ought to pray. That prayer goes up at the altar of incense before God as a sweet-smelling aroma because the Holy Spirit prays through us, making intercession for us. (See Romans 8.)

He's praying on our behalf, interceding for us. On top of the mercy seat, the blood was sprinkled once a year for the remission of our sins. Where the angels are facing each other declaring, "Holy! Holy! Holy!" and the glory of God shows up in the midst of that, and God grants mercy. He grants mercy! God sits on the mercy seat, not the judgment throne.

Underneath that mercy seat is the ark of the covenant, containing three things that speak to us today: the Ten Commandments, which remind us that God has supernaturally inscribed on your heart who you are and who you ought to be; the pot of manna, which reminds us that God supernaturally provides for us in every situation; and Aaron's rod that budded, which reminds us of that God is supernaturally gracious to us, bringing forth His fruit in our lives because we're connected to Him in prayer.

"Prayer is not learned in a classroom but in a closet."

E. M. Bounds said, "Prayer is not learned in a classroom but in a closet." You could read all day about how to pray, but you'll only learn how to pray by starting to pray. Prayer is like driving. You don't learn how to drive by reading a book on it and listening to a podcast about brake pedals and gas pedals. No, you learn to drive by driving. Similarly, you learn how to pray by praying.

← LEAVE THE PHONE ALONE AND GO TO THE THRONE. →

Prayer is the lifting of your life, all its problems and all its joys, back up to God. When you lift it up to God, God will breathe on it, and God will fix it so that it can go onward. It starts inward, it goes outward, we lift it upward, and then it can go onward. When you pray, a revival wind begins to blow gently in your soul until sometimes a hurricane is created, and God will blow things out of your way. I just come as a reminder to you that whenever you need a real turn around in your life, it's prayer time! If you get in a prayer closet and allow the power of the Holy Spirit to begin to move in you, something supernatural and divine will happen.

God will begin to blow things out of your mind that you couldn't cleanse on your own accord. There are some things that God has reserved only for Himself. You can't do everything that needs to be done for you. There are some things that God wrote into the script where God says, "This is My part. This is where I come in, and you can't come in to do your next part until I come in and do My part. When I enter the stage of your life, I'll rise up and make Myself known." When life knocks you to your knees, you're in a perfect position to pray. When life knocks you to your knees, don't just run to the phone to call your best friend, or your mommy, or your pastor. Leave the phone alone and go to the throne. You've got some issues now that you've got to go to the throne of grace!

When life is whirling around you, changing dramatically, more than you ever thought it could—take it to the throne of grace.

15

How to Resolve Problems

Changing your trajectory will cause unexpected problems. Even when you're doing all the right things, working hard, praying hard, stressing enough but not too much, even then you'll still encounter unexpected problems. Sometimes the problem comes from you—which means that you also have the power to change it. Sometimes the problem comes from the devil—which means that God will visit His deliverance on you. But sometimes the problems come from God, and it's because He's just trying to grow us.

We look around the world and think that the problems are too big—but really, we're just too small, so God has a way of using problems to grow us. Adversity is the best friend of those who desire to do better...because your trials come to make you strong. They will strengthen something in you.

God's Process

Let me give you a window into God's process—a sneak peak at how He grows us. First, there's a need for change or growth. You're stuck in a rut, you're living in sin, or you're just ready for the next step of sanctification. And so, second, God uses a crisis. The word *crisis* means "turning point." God has to use the crisis, something to turn you from the way you are originally headed, or else you'll wind up at the bottom of the mountain instead of the top. He has to create a crisis when He wants to turn you.

Third, the crisis creates a hunger for answers. Have you ever been in a problem, and the pain that the problem is producing in your life is so intense that it makes you start questioning stuff? You start questioning the very nature of who you are, and who God is, and you start asking questions like, "What am I doing here? Should I leave or should I stay?" Have you ever been there? Where you got into something, and it looked like it was good at the onset, but then you ran into some problems, and it started hurting you, and you started wondering, "Should I throw in the towel or should I tough it out?" You start looking for information. You start looking for answers. You start looking for help.

Finally, the hunger for answers brings revelation from God; He promised, "*Seek, and ye shall find*" (Matthew 7:7 KJV). That's the good news of the gospel, that if we confess our sins, He is faithful and just to forgive us our sins and cleanse us from all unrighteousness. (See 1 John 1:9.) Every problem is linked to sin, but God will cleanse us not just from our sin, but also from all the unrighteousness around us. It means that He will grow us, whenever we have a problem, in order to overcome our problem. Problems stretch us. Whenever you solve a problem, you arrive at a different level of knowledge, authority, and responsibility.

Maintain the Right Perspective

But how do you solve the problems? Begin with the right perspective. Remember that just by its definition, a problem is that which can be solved. Marilyn Voss Savant said, "Being defeated is often a temporary condition but giving up is what makes it permanent." It may not be solved immediately, but it can be solved.

Also remember that it's the problems of your life that lead to your development. It's like a photographer's dark room. You're exposed to the negative, and your brain will develop it in your life. Dark moments in your life become your dark room. The photographs of your life develop there, so learn to embrace the dark moments because they actually help to develop you even though you're the only one who sees it.

IF IT WAS OVERNIGHT SUCCESS, THEN IT WAS A LONG, LONG NIGHT!

It just looks like it happened overnight because you seem to develop overnight, but what happened is that you developed in the dark. You get ready for some carrots, you don't see the carrots growing on top of the ground. It's underground. You only see a little green foliage, but the real development is happening under the surface. A champion does not show up in the ring; that's not where champions are made, that's where they are exposed. They were *made* back in the gym just practicing in and out, over and over, day by day, diligently, consistently.

Nobody sees you staying up late at night trying to figure out what in the world you're going to do, and how you're going to pay for this and juggle that, and robbing Peter to pay Paul. Everybody thinks that you are big-balling but they don't see you staying up at night asking, *How do I pay my car note and my house note and my rent and keep all of this stuff?* Everybody is thinking that your success was overnight. If it was overnight success, then it was a long, long night!

So maintain the right perspective, and remember that greatness is always developed in the dark days. In desperate times, more than anything else, people need perspective. Why? Because perspective brings calm—and calm leads to clear thinking. Clear thinking yields new ideas, and ideas produce the blossom of an answer. You've got to maintain the right perspective.

Maintain the Right Attitude

Never make your problems about yourself. That's for narcissistic people who are the center of their own universe, who think that everything in the whole world revolves around them and that it's always got to be about them. A major cause of negative thinking and poor mental health is self-absorption, just being consumed with yourself. Selfishness ultimately hurts not only the people around a self-centered person, but the selfish person himself.

YOUR OUTLOOK DETERMINES YOUR OUTCOME.

Someone once asked a very distinguished psychiatrist, Dr. Karl Menninger, "What would you advise a person to do if he felt a nervous breakdown coming on?" Most expected him to reply, "You should consult a psychiatrist," but he didn't. To their astonishment, Dr. Menninger replied: "Lock up your house, go across the railway tracks, find someone in need, and do something to help that person."

Now isn't that interesting? In order to save your mind, help somebody else. See, when you give help to somebody else, God will send it back and it blesses you. That's why the Bible says that it is more blessed to give than it is to receive. When you give, you receive the gift of joy, of peace, of purpose, of accomplishment, of meaning and understanding in your own life. Do you realize that generous people are rarely ever mentally ill? Keep your attitude outward-focused, and you'll keep from swallowing yourself in depression. Always remember that your outlook determines your outcome.

Identify Your Problem

If you don't know what your problem is, you can't treat it! Figure out what is actually wrong. There are some folks that have so many problems; they've got this and they've got that, and they don't exactly know the problem. What you thought was one problem might actually be six different problems that look like they're connected, but they're not! You can't expect to win unless you know why you lost.

Distinguish your problem from a fact of life. Is this something that can be changed, or is it a fact of life that no amount of effort will alter? You need to know when to fight, and when to accept. Don't waste your time trying to change a fact of life. Shift your focus and then look for other opportunities. If you're born a woman, you're going to be a woman. Just deal with it. If you're a man, you're going to be a man. It's a fact of life, but don't make the fact of life your problem. It is what it is. If you're from a certain race, you can't help that. God made you, and He doesn't make any mistakes.

Allow Problems to Trigger Solutions

The size of your problem predicts the size of your future. If you've got a big future, you'll have big problems. There was a man down in the Florida named David Miller. He had a restaurant business there, and he had so many folks coming in to his business that he started having a problem with people waiting to be seated. It dawned on him, "Why don't I create some kind of a paging system where a person doesn't have to stand around but can be given a pager, and when their table is ready it'll buzz?"

Out of his problem came an answer. He developed a paging system that would vibrate to let people know when their table was ready. He started making more money selling his paging system to 25,000 other restaurants and country clubs. It started doing bigger business than his restaurant was doing. In fact, he started doing so well that Motorola got into his idea. It's amazing how God let his problem predict the size of his future. What he thought was a problem he turned into an opportunity, and God blessed his life. I'm just telling you that hidden in every problem and crisis is an opportunity for you.

Did you know that a woman named Mary Anderson invented windshield wipers? She was on a tram in New York on a wintry day, and the tram had to stop every few minutes so the driver could get out and push snow off the windshield. So to solve the problem, she invented windshield wipers—and they work for rain as well as snow!

Or how about the dishwasher? It was invented by a woman named Josephine Cochran, who happened to be a woman of means. She had servants washing her dishes, but besides being slow, the servants were breaking some of her fine china. So she invented a dishwashing machine.

These situations might have only frustrated most of us, but these ladies knew that a *problem* is the seedbed for a *solution*. If you're frustrated by a problem situation, don't get mad; get smart. Let your frustration drive you to productivity. Produce something out of that difficulty.

There was a lady named Betty Nesmith Graham. She was a typist, but she wasn't a very good typist, and she lived before the days of the oh-so-handy backspace button! She was doing the old kind of typing, on a typewriter, where if you messed up, you had to retype the whole page. Betty Nesmith got sick and tired of pulling the paper out and starting all over again. One day, she was watching house painters who, when they messed up, would just paint over their mistake. *Hmmm.* She invented Liquid Paper, so that she could paint over her mistakes, too, without retyping her whole sheet.

Necessity is the mother of invention. If you've got something that has been vexing you, the very problem that frustrates you out of your wits is often the very problem God has ordained for you to solve and bring a helpful new idea or concept into being. You'll honestly be surprised!

When you're dealing with those situations of difficulty and adversity, the key to finding a solution or an answer is often to simply recognize a higher law at work. Allow me to illustrate: we know that water freezes at 32 degrees Fahrenheit. That's a physical law; I didn't make it up. Water was freezing at 32 degrees Fahrenheit long before I was ever around. Meanwhile, water boils at 212 degrees Fahrenheit. I didn't make that one up either; that, too, is a law of physics.

But do you know what happens when you add salt to water? Salt water doesn't freeze at 32 degrees; it's got to get much colder than that before it will freeze. And if you heat up a pot of salt water, the temperature must be hotter than 212 degrees before it will boil.

Now does that mean that the physical law of water freezing at 32 degrees, and the physical law of water boiling at 212 degrees, are both invalid laws? No it doesn't. It simply means that you're encountering *higher* laws that come into effect when salt is added to the water.

Now think about that in relation to the fact that Jesus has called us the salt of the earth. So we're operating by a higher law, by the Holy Spirit within us. Our love doesn't grow cold like that of others, because we live by a higher law. Our tempers don't reach a rapid boiling point like that of other people, because we're living by a higher law. And by that higher law, we've been changed by the power of the Spirit.

So whenever you encounter situations down here that are problematic and difficult, look for the higher law. There's a higher law that will take you out of that, a higher law that will defy our normal expectations.

PROBLEMS

So to sum up, I want to give you a little acronym that you can put on your fridge: PROBLEMS. "P" is for "Predictors." Your problems are predictors, helping to mold your future. "R" is for "Reminders." Problems remind us that we cannot succeed alone. Problems remind us that we might need to ask somebody for help, mentorship, advice, or direction. Then the "O" is for "Opportunities." Problems pull us out of ruts and prompt us to think creatively; every problem contains a built-in opportunity. Learn to look for the opportunity.

"B" is for "Blessings." Problems are sometimes opening doors that we otherwise would not walk through. "L" is for "Lessons." Problems provide us instruction with each new challenge; every problem is a school. You need to learn the lesson of that school before you leave that problem so that when you encounter a similar problem, it is no longer a problem because you've got some answers! "E" is for "Everywhere"—because problems are everywhere. They're not just confined to one place. We don't just have problems in government and school systems and Fortune 500 companies. If you've got a mom and pop operation, you're going to have problems. If you've got just one child, you're going to have problems. If you've got twelve children, you're going to have problems. M is for "Messages." Messages warn us about potential disaster.

And then, finally, I love the last letter on PROBLEMS. It is S, which stands for "Solvable." Every problem has a solution—that's the good news of the gospel! God uses our problems to direct us, inspect us, correct us, protect us, and perfect us.

Remember that problems are normal to life. Don't think that you were the first one to have it, and don't think you'll be the last. Who told you that you wouldn't have problems once you were saved? The truth of the matter is that when God comes into your life, it doesn't mean that you won't have problems. It simply means problems won't have you.

16

How to Work

The huge changes that have the most impact on our lives often seem to relate to the loss of a job or a major job change. Because of the dynamism of the American economy, fully twenty million jobs are lost or restructured every year. Twenty million! That's a whole lot of people's lives being disrupted. The good news is that millions of jobs are also created each year. And consider this: according to the *USA TODAY* data analytics, by 2017, an estimated 2.5 million new, middle-skill jobs will be added to the workforce.[8] That represents a lot of potential opportunities.

Now, we need all the opportunities we can get. There was a time when the typical person's career goal was to get hired by a good company, work there for forty years, and receive a gold watch upon retirement. But now the typical person could have a dozen different jobs and three to five different careers.

Many companies are no longer looking for long-term employees. They want to have you for a couple of years, maximize your output while you're still at a relatively low rate of pay, and then get rid of you and hire somebody else who's young and creative and innovative, and start the process over again. They can pay a cheaper salary to that

---

8. MaryJo Webster, "Where the Jobs Are," *USA TODAY*, www.usatoday.com/story/news/nation/2014/09/30/job-economy-middle-skill-growth-wage-blue-collar/14797413/ (accessed 22 April 2015).

person instead of paying out your raises according to your seniority, and that helps keep their business lean and mean. It's just the way the game works. So you've got to be prepared for that.

Meanwhile, because of unstable economic conditions, changing consumer tastes, and worldwide competition, entire industries are often downsized or even eliminated. Sometimes the demand for people within a particular classification or career may decline or even disappear after a few short years. Many of the manufacturing jobs in the U.S. have been shipped overseas to China, India, or Brazil. We've witnessed the transition from physical labor to mind labor as the dominant employee activity in the U.S.

In his essay entitled "Self-Esteem in the Information Age," psychologist Nathaniel Branden makes these observations:

> We now live in a global economy characterized by rapid change, accelerating scientific and technological breakthroughs, and an unprecedented level of competitiveness. These developments create demands for higher levels of education and training than were required of previous generations. Everyone acquainted with business culture knows this. What is not equally understood is that these developments also create new demands on our psychological resources. Specifically, these developments ask for a greater capacity for innovation, self-management, personal responsibility, and self-direction....Today, organizations need not only a higher level of knowledge and skill among all those who participate but also a higher level of independence, self-reliance, self-trust, and the capacity to exercise initiative.[9]

In other words, employers are looking for self-starters, innovative folks, people who can be productive while working without close supervision. We've got so many opportunities now in a number of career fields to have more autonomy, to work from home and telecommute, but you've

---

9. Nathaniel Branden, "Self-Esteem in the Information Age," Red Barn, mol.redbarn. org/objectivism/Writing/NathanielBranden/SelfEsteemInTheInformationAge.html (accessed 22 February 2015).

got to be mature enough to be able to handle that. Some folks are like, "If I'm at home, I'm going to get up late, eat constantly, and be posting, pinning, and tweeting all day." That won't fly! You need self-discipline, a strong sense of responsibility, plenty of self-motivation, and the quick ability to produce results. Companies are looking for people that they can trust to be able to work in an environment all by themselves. They're looking for workers who don't need a line supervisor looking over their shoulder every five minutes. If the money ever gets tight in the organization, guess who's the first to go: the very folks that have been slacking and who have been difficult to manage.

To effectively position yourself for advancement in this ever-changing marketplace, there are a few principles you ought to incorporate into your mind-set and into your behavior.

Clarity

Perhaps your most important responsibility is to have clarity. You've got to see the end of a thing from the beginning. If your vision isn't clear, you won't recognize that vision when you get to it, and you won't be able to explain it to others. That's what a leader's responsibility is: to have vision, and to share the vision with others.

← ─────────────────────────

CAN YOUR VISION FIT ON A T-SHIRT?

─────────────────────────→

Clarity is the ability to see reality and to acknowledge, "This is the way it is." You must be absolutely clear about who you are, what you stand for, and what you're called to do. Your vision must be clear. If I have to read five pages explaining your vision, you obviously don't know it well enough yourself! If you can't express it in a sentence or two, your vision isn't clear enough. Can your vision fit on a T-shirt? If it can, then you know you have a clear vision.

For me, my purpose and vision is simply to go out and to make Jesus known—it's very simple! I'm not twisted or confused about it at all. Our church's slogan for a number of years has been this: "Reaching the lost; teaching the found." It's the essence of what we are as a church—evangelistic in nature to reach the lost, having a passion for souls, and having a compassion in Christ to then teach the found. That's clarity.

Be clear about what you want. They say the man who wears two watches is never really sure what time it is. So be clear and simple and *confident* about your vision; be sure about that one thing. Know exactly what you're called in the Lord to do.

Competence

Set a standard of excellence in the place where you work, and in all that you do. Be competent. Be able to do the job that you're hired to do and asked to do.

Seek ways to improve the quality of whatever product or service your company provides. Martin Luther King Jr. said that if a man was a street sweeper, he should sweep that street as well as Michelangelo painted or Beethoven composed. "Do it so well," he said, "that nobody living, dead, or yet unborn could sweep it any better." He also said, "If you can't be the tallest pine on the top of the hill, be the best little shrub in the valley."

It's all about being competent in what God has gifted and called you to be. Whatever it is, there's something God has uniquely qualified you for. You have to be able to operate in your strength zone, in your area of competence. In whatever area you work, you want to be someone who gets things done. That's why it's always important to stay connected to those who are on a level beyond where you currently are, and to keep improving your performance.

If you're working for a company or organization right now, and if you're a really great worker, finish all your work and then go to your supervisor and say, "I'm finished with the assignment you gave me. Is there anything else I can do for you?" At first they may start giving you some busy work, but if you get right to it immediately and finish that busy work, and then come back to that person for more—eventually you'll develop a reputation with that boss. And he'll say to others in leadership, "If you need something done, I know just the person who'll do it," and they'll call on you.

Commitment

You also want to demonstrate compassionate commitment to whatever organization you're working for. Your commitment motivates and inspires other people to do their best work and to put their whole heart into their jobs.

You cannot depend on uncommitted people. So be dependable. Show that you're committed. That commitment will include a commitment to your own place of responsibility within that company or organization, and a commitment to making yourself more valuable to them.

COMMITMENT COMES FROM CONVICTION.

Remember that commitment always comes from a conviction. If you lack conviction on the inside, you will lack commitment on the outside. You can't just wake up one morning and decide to be committed at work; no, it has to come from an inner conviction that you are called to be where you are, and that you are called to be the best employee that you possibly can.

And let me also note that you can always learn big things by the little things that people are willing to do—or not to do. I'll never forget a friend of mine, who, before we were friends, heard me on TBN making the statement that "if a person is too big to preach in a small place, then they're too small to preach in a big place." So after he heard me say that on TV, he called me up and said, "I'm a pastor in a small place. I want to see if you'll come." He wanted to call me on the carpet about it—but I surprised him. I went!

Constraints

Identify the constraints or the limiting factors that will determine the speed at which you can achieve your goals and carry out your vision and calling. Your constraints are the borders of your life or the parameters within which you operate. You've got to set limits for yourself so that you never compromise your character or your integrity. You must have constraints so that you stay in your lane.

In the 2012 Olympics, there was a runner who finished an event in fifth place, but still brought home the bronze medal. Why? Because both the third-place finisher and the fourth-place finisher were disqualified for stepping out of their lanes during the race. They needed to conform to their constraints.

If you're going to do something really well in your life, you need constraints to help you resist the temptation to do something *else* that seems good. A broken focus will keep you from achieving your goal. That's why you have to put blinders on things that constrain your focus and tell you, "I'm going full force in this direction. This is my goal. I can't get involved right now in these other things on the side."

I know gifted people who have great competence, and they're fully committed, but they get distracted because they don't have sufficient constraints. They let their focus get drawn away from what they should be doing.

Creativity

Remain open to new ideas from all sources. Did you know that one of the best places to get new ideas is from complainers? Find complaining people—you won't have to look very far—and hear them out. If you want to know how to create something that becomes better than what the competition has, find somebody who's complaining about what the competition is doing, and you'll learn how you can successfully compete against them.

FIND COMPLAINING PEOPLE AND HEAR THEM OUT.

When you don't have a whole lot of money, you'd be surprised how creative that can force you to become. You have to get by with less, so you find creative ways to do exactly that. You end up getting more with less. There's nothing that will stimulate creativity faster than being broke. That's when you get real creative. The less money you have, the more creative you're forced to be. Necessity is the mother of invention!

Creativity often produces its best work when you're all alone and can't depend on others. So you find creative ways to get things done yourself. You are going to have some situations where you are going to be making lemonade, and you are going to end up putting too much sugar in it. You know how to fix that; add some more water and lemon to it. If you run out of material making a dress, make a blouse instead. Then wear some black pants with it. Improvise. You've got to be flexible to adjust.

You can do just about anything you set your mind to, if you give enough time to it. Everything you say you can't do is because you haven't invested the time to learn to do it. If you put sufficient time into it, you can master it. You can work your way through any challenging situation you face; with the help of a creative mind you'll find a way out. So you never want to lose creativity, because it's such a gift when you're in a bind.

Proverbs 18:16 tells us, "A man's gift makes room for him." There's a creative gift within you that will make so much room for you. Use your gift. Focus on your gift. Get in tune with God, who gave you that gift, and start working on that gift. Practice it, and release it for serving and blessing others.

Creative ideas often come when you're sitting somewhere all by yourself. God will give you ideas for creative inventions, designs, and discoveries when your mind is less distracted. If you really want to see your creativity in full force, find a spot alone with our creative God and allow His thoughts to flow, so that they flow through you. Creativity flows in isolation.

Consistency

Develop the self-discipline to be consistent—dependable, reliable, calm, and predictable in all situations. People are afraid to trust those whose reactions they cannot predict. When there's a storm, they need to know you're not going to be blown away by the wind.

If you struggle with managing your anger, they won't be putting you in a supervisory position at work. They'll be afraid to trust you, because they never know when you'll demonstrate inconsistency in your temperament. Even-keeled folks are the ones who are most often placed in positions of responsibility. So you can't let every little thing that comes your way be such a distraction to you that you get all keyed up and feel you're about to lose your mind.

When you get angry, your creativity shuts down. When you get frustrated, creativity is stopped in its tracks. When your mind is frustrated, you can't think. It's as though somebody has thrown a monkey wrench into the programming of your mind, and your thoughts are disordered. So watch yourself and make sure you're consistent in your life.

You need a calm, steady mind to be able to think under pressure. If you're in an airplane that's suddenly losing altitude at a furious rate, you may hear the pilot announcing, "Please remain calm," but your life is flashing before your eyes! You don't want to remain calm! However, if you lose your head in an emergency situation like that, it will only mean that more people will die or be injured because they're too terrified and flustered to follow instructions. They panic, and when you panic, you die. So remember: although you may be about to die, screaming is not going to help. So keep telling yourself, *Stay calm.*

Take a deep breath. I know your situation may be frightening and painful, but let God come into that situation, and He'll lead you through it.

Continuous Learning

Allow me to emphasize again the importance of continuous learning. Be committed to reading, to listening, to upgrading your personal knowledge and skills.

Set aside time for this. Set aside resources to invest for training and development. The best companies are those that have the best trained people. The second best companies have the second best trained people. And those that train the least are on their way out of business.

LEARNERS WILL ALWAYS BEAT THE LEARNED.

As times change, commit to becoming a perpetual learner. Let me say this to you: *Learners* will always beat the so-called *learned*, the people who got their degree (or their degrees) but then let their education stop there. Eric Hoffer wrote, "In a time of drastic change it is the learners who inherit the future. The learned usually find themselves equipped to live in a world that no longer exists."[10] You've got to be a student of life, constantly learning about things in this world.

---

10. Eric Hoffer, *Reflections on the Human Condition*, (New York City: Harper & Row, 1973), Section 32.

You've got to make a determination to continue to learn throughout your life. Always work on *you*. Continue to develop yourself. Find ways to make yourself better. Get around other people who are on a higher level than you are.

Connections

You don't get the best jobs by surfing the net. The best jobs happen through networking, through meeting people. Eighty percent of the best-paying jobs come by reference of somebody that you meet—a human being just like yourself who meets you, likes you, and then puts in a recommendation for you.

The only reason that people with big money haven't invested in you is simply that they don't know you. If they knew you, and what your potential is, maybe they would invest in you. People invest in the people they know.

So you have to get out. The Internet is only *artificial intelligence*—and the operative word there is *artificial*. Virtual reality is *not* real; virtual reality is *un*real. If you think you've got 1,200 friends because that's what Facebook tells you—get real! Ask all of them to send you ten dollars, as a real friend would be willing to do, and see what happens. I find that folks invest in people that they know. So you have to get out and you have to meet people in the real world because we don't live in cyberspace. You don't eat in cyberspace. You've got to do that in the real world. Don't send me a cyber piece of chicken! No, I want the real thing. Cyber fruit doesn't do it for you. You've got to have the real thing.

Make the most of your *real* connections with people, the face-to-face connections. Work hard for those who are your supervisors and managers, and show them your genuine desire to be a learner. Someday you may hear them say, "I see something in you that I can teach. I can train you for this. You've got a teachable spirit. I can use you. I can help you. I can make you what you need to be."

Go the Extra Mile

Excellent people go the extra mile. When you get ready to go to your office, show up early—not just for the interview or just on the first day. You be willing to get there early and to stay there late.

Once you've got in there and have done your work, be willing to help some of your coworkers if they need help. Find out your supervisor or boss's heart and just go to them and let them know, "Listen if you ever need anybody to come in on a Saturday and help you to rearrange the furniture in the office call me. I am the person. Call me." Be willing to come early, stay late, and go the extra mile. It will separate you from what everybody else is doing.

Other folks, if they get off at 5:00 p.m., they start getting ready at 4:15 p.m. They clean up their workstation, shut down their brains, and don't answer the phone. I have been there. In one place I worked at that closed at five, there was a lady who would start cleaning off her desk, putting stuff in drawers, and fetching her pocketbook at 4:15. She was ready to get out of there. She was on her mark, ready-set-go, at 4:55.

Some folks are just there to get their check. They are not really there to help serve people. But if you're willing to go the extra mile, I promise you, will always be noticed. I don't mean just by your coworkers, but also by your supervisors and managers and owners. Go the extra mile in your personal life, too! Do more than is expected of you. I mean, if somebody lets you use their car, don't just refuel it; get it washed before returning it. Set higher expectations for yourself than what other people or the situation around you might dictate.

And when you are willing to do more, don't ask for a handout: "Are you going to pay me for this? How much you gonna pay me?" What happened to the Boy Scouts that used to help old ladies across the street and help you bring your groceries in? You go the extra mile, and you will be rewarded. There are some things that you pay in first. You are sowing seeds. You will eventually reap it; don't worry about that.

My wife lovingly taught me the handy "also principle." When you pull your clothes off hang them up *also*. When you pull off your shoes—put them away *also*. When you finish eating dinner, take your plate and put it in the sink *also*. It's just going the extra mile for someone you love. My wife and I have a habit that when we go to a restaurant, we will start stacking dishes after we have eaten. We are not paid to do that at all; but it's a part of the "also" principle.

When my wife's bagging her groceries at the store, she'll turn to the customer next to her and help that customer bag groceries, too. I'll tell her, "You don't work here!" But she's a creature of the "also" principle. It doesn't have to be an either/or principle; let it be an *also* principle. Whatever I was going to do, add something on it *also*. I don't just take the grocery cart out to the car, remove my groceries, and leave the cart out in the parking lot to put a ding in somebody's car until an employee picks it up. I always take it back. Sometimes I am fussing in my mind like, "They need to put more cart corrals in here because I have to walk a half mile to return this thing!" but because I used the cart I am going to return it *also*.

You might not think much about that, but when an employee sees you helping out, it will begin to speak volumes about who you are. Now I know this may not be deeply spiritual but if somebody sees that I have gone beyond the call of duty, and I have actually helped them to do their job when I am not getting paid, I am sowing seed—and you never sow seed without a return coming.

See we are born of an incorruptible seed, and an incorruptible seed is a seed that never fails to produce a harvest. You are sowing seeds, and that's part of a character of excellence, which is an essential part of changing your trajectory. Excellence is a habit. You don't just do it because somebody is looking at you; I find myself doing it even if I am all by myself. I went to one restaurant and they served these peanuts as a little appetizer. Customers are supposed to just push all the peanut shells onto the floor. I was eating some peanuts, and I was stacking mine neatly on the side of the table. I told the waitress that brushing them on the floor goes against the grain of all of my home training.

But then the waitress came over and pushed them on the floor anyway! Like I said, sowing seeds *usually* pays off....

The workplace is filled with unprecedented changes these days, but by depending on the Lord and following His principles and wisdom, you'll see Him open up a career path for you that will astonish you. God is faithful!

17

How to Praise

Do you know what attitude you're trying to have as you begin to change your trajectory?

Your attitude ought to be an attitude of praise. I cannot tell you the number of people who have been able to change their trajectory because they learned how to transcend their problems by praising God. They thanked God almost as a down payment (in advance) for what they had prayed about. When you praise God *before* you get the answer, it is one of the greatest manifestations that you believe that God has already granted the thing that you have petitioned Him about. It's a great sign of faith.

Two Parts to Praise

I love how Hebrews 13:15–16 talks about praise: *"Therefore, by Him [Jesus Christ] let us continually offer the sacrifice of praise to God— that is the fruit of our lips giving thanks to His name. But do not forget to do good and to share for with such sacrifice God is well pleased."* Now notice something about these two particular verses. It talks about praise being the fruit of our lips giving thanks to His name, and it calls praise a sacrifice here—the sacrifice of praise to God. Are sacrifices easy? No, they hurt you a bit; they cost you a bit. So your praise might sometimes be a sacrifice because you may not always feel like doing it, but make it a sacrifice. God honors sacrifice.

PRAISE IS MORE THAN LIP SERVICE— IT'S LIFE SERVICE.

Praise is the fruit of our lips giving thanks to His name. When we just thank Him and say, "Lord, I thank You for changing my trajectory," it is the fruit of your lips giving thanks to His name. You'll be surprised how a spirit of revival will begin to bubble up on the inside of you because you are giving praise unto His name. However, that's not your only responsibility. The other sacrifice that is an integral part of praise is noted here in verse 16, *"And do not forget to do good...."* When you do good that's when you get praise. Do not forget to do good!

Not all praise is verbal. Praise is also doing good and sharing. *"Do not forget to do good and to share for with such sacrifices, God is well pleased."* Remember that faith without works is dead. Praise is more than lip service—it's life service. So our praise should not merely be audible; our praise should be visible.

I wish more church people knew that, understood it, and applied it as a two-winged bird. Too many of them flap the wing of just verbal praise (the fruit of their lips giving thanks unto God). They can bless God all day long with their lips, but that's only one wing of praise, and you can't get off the ground flapping one wing. We were designed to bless God's name, but we also need the other wing, to do good and to share with others.

Did you know that when you do good to help other people, you actually feel good about that? It blesses you. When you bless somebody by cleaning their house, or giving a little money so they can eat a square meal, it not only releases positive endorphins in the recipient of the blessing, but also creates a positive experience in the one who gives the blessing. That's why the Bible teaches it is more blessed to give than to receive. When you give the gift (the blessing) to someone else, they receive it, but when you as a giver give it, you receive the gift of joy. You receive that, and it causes you to praise God because He was able to use you.

We need to praise Him both with the fruit of our lips, giving thanks to His name, and also in doing good and sharing with other individuals. Our churches should be balanced toward our families and communities because God calls us to be a people who will not only represent a strong vertical relationship in verbal praise upwardly to God, but also doing good and sharing horizontally some of the blessings that we have received. When you get the vertical in addition to the horizontal, you form the way of the cross. It is the way of the cross. That is not a coincidence! It connects people to God, and it helps bring heaven down to earth through what God has done in your heart.

Motive for Praise

We praise God because we know He is fearful and great. Do you know the Bible injunction that says, "Fear the Lord your God"? In the Hebrew, it's really a reminder to see the invisible because the Hebrew word for "fear the Lord" actually means *seeing*. So think of it this way: to *see* the Lord is to *fear* Him.

Some people have no fear as long as their boss isn't around. They do whatever they want, and act however they please. It's almost like when the cat is away, the mice will play, but that is not how we can treat the Lord! We fear Him and walk and live reverently, soberly, and discreetly in the fear of God because we see Him through our spiritual eyes. We see that God is with us.

If you can't see God, you lose your fear of Him because you think that you're hiding, you think that you can get away with something. So my admonition to you today is to never let God out of your sight. And that's why we praise Him: praise brings the focus back to God, so that we see Him. It keeps us with a God-consciousness on the inside so we can see Him. If you let God get out of your sight, you will start living like there is no God.

Too many people use praise as a tool to try to manipulate God to bless them. I've been to some places, and they're like, "Come on! Praise Him! Praise Him! If you'll praise Him, God will give you anything you want!" Praise is not a tool of manipulation in order to get what you want from God. It's not our whole idea of where we are stroking God's ego. That's manipulative, and manipulation is evil and wicked. Manipulation is pretending that you are right to get something that's wrong. It's using a wrong motive and pretense in order to get something. It is moving a person to believe that you are one way so that you tap into what motivates them…to get it out of them.

We cannot use praise to stroke God's ego so that He gives us a new car. As if that would even work! He's God, after all. God can see through you. He knows your thoughts and desires, the very intent of your thoughts. He knows the intent of your manipulation. If you give something just to be seen by people, do you think that you're really fooling God? No, God knows if you have given something just to be seen; He knows if you've just done something nice just so somebody will pat you on the back and say, "Oh what a wonderful person this is!" The Bible says that when you do good, you already have your reward with you. So it's impossible to fool God because God knows your motive. The Word is a discerner of the thoughts and intents of the heart.

Praise Can Change the World

Praise changes the atmosphere. If you walk into a room and things are cold toward you, but you walk in anyway, encouraging people and giving generous yet genuine praise, the whole atmosphere of the room will change. Try it and see! In most places you go, whether it's a family or a business or what have you, people are not appreciated sufficiently. You'd be surprised at the number of people who never take the time to stop a person and say, "Thank you so much for what you do."

I've seen people in restaurants who, when the waiter brings them additional water or another requested item, will just keep on in their conversation and never acknowledge the waiter. If somebody has just served you, it really doesn't take a whole lot out of you to acknowledge that person with gratitude to say, "Thank you. You know what? I appreciate you for really being on top of things here. You have not allowed my glass to get empty one time...." When there are bad things, people are certainly generous with pointing out flaws and criticisms. So why aren't we generous with our gratitude?

THE DEVIL IS ALLERGIC TO PRAISE.

Praise is a powerful, powerful thing. It's not just some nice quote covered in flowers on a Pinterest board. Praise is a weapon of war! I'm telling you, the devil is allergic to praise. He just can't stand it when God is getting glory; it angers him. The devil is your biggest hater, and he can't stand to see you having a good time. You're saying, "Praise the Lord! The Lord has blessed me!" It really irritates the devil to see you giving praise to your Maker.

Praise is a counterattack against the devil and his minions who would try to make you curse, both the devil and his minions. Praise focuses not only on the magnificence of who God is but also on what He has done. Praise is not based on what you are waiting on God to do. You praise God for who He is and what He has already done.

People who get frustrated and angry with God are focusing on what they are waiting on God to do instead of what He has already done for them. Think about the last time you were in a jam, and God came through for you. That's when praise will begin to bubble up in your heart. I'm reminding you that it is time for a focus shift in your life. If you've been focusing on all the stuff you are waiting for God to do for you—open this career opportunity, give me this house and this car, make my husband or my wife like this or that—you'll never get around to actually praising God.

But, on the other hand, when you have a heart of gratitude over what God has already brought into your life, it creates a bridge over which future blessings will be brought. So you take the gratitude (the praises of God) in your life and give them liberally back to Him. It's time for a focus shift now. When you begin to think of God's grace toward you, it will cause a spirit of praise to come in your heart because you realize that God does love you with an incredible love.

Job's Praise

Have you noticed that after Job lost all ten of his children and most of his servants and livestock, instead of focusing on all the stuff he had lost, he praised God? Job declared it boldly in Job 1:22, "*Naked came I from my mother's womb and naked I shall return there. The* LORD *gave and the* LORD *has taken away. Blessed be the name of the* LORD!" It's like, "I've lost everything that I had but blessed be the name of the Lord!"

He blessed God even amid the loss because the Bible says, "*In everything give thanks*" (1 Thessalonians 5:18). It doesn't say to give thanks *for* everything—nobody in their right mind would praise God for ten children dying! But it says to give thanks *in* everything. Job was still praising God because God is still worthy to be praised even if a loved one dies.

Job had the right perspective, so Job stayed loyal in his heart toward God. Even when Job was afflicted to the degree that he lost his health and was left with nothing but a nagging wife that told him, "You ought to just curse God and die because your life is jacked up!" he still did not stop praising God. Now, you may also feel like your life is jacked up and in shambles because of your credit, indebtedness, or children that you might have fathered or mothered, and you're wondering, "God, what in the world can I do? What do I have in my life to praise God about?"

But if you look around, you can always find somebody in a worse condition than where you are. There are people in other countries who would love to change places with you. They've never even had the stuff that you've enjoyed and gotten in debt over. God's able to deliver you. He's still able to deliver you. Is anything really too hard for God? God is still worthy to be praised.

The Bible says that Job was an upright man...and eschewed evil. The very time that we begin to have negative things happen to us, we start wondering within ourselves, *What did I do to cause this calamity to happen in my life? Maybe God is punishing me for my sin.* Have you not read the Bible in Psalm 34:19? *"Many are the afflictions of the righteous, but the LORD delivers him out of them all."* You may not have done anything wrong, and yet bad stuff can still happen to you. The great challenge here, the great test here, is whether you will be faithful to still praise God. Can you still praise Him?

Job that came to that place in his own life where he said, *"Though He slay me, yet will I trust Him"* (Job 13:15). I love just that little pivot word *yet*. A little three-letter word changed his whole attitude. There are too many people that focus on the fact that God slayed them. Really they are blaming God for allowing them to be slayed. They say, *"Though He slay me,"* and they're stuck on that part. Job continued, *"Yet will I trust Him because I know God still loves me."*

The devil said to God, "You know Your folks who love You and serve You only do it because You bless them, but if You take away their blessing I bet You they would curse You." God said, "I bet they won't. If anybody really loves Me and knows Me because they're connected to Me, I can take the stuff. It's not about the stuff; it's about Me...." God said, "Let's test somebody." The Lord said, *"Have you considered My servant, Job?"* (Job 1:8). He knew that Job was a righteous man; one that walked uprightly and eschewed evil. So it was a demonstration. He told the devil, "All right. You do all this but don't touch his soul." Job lost all ten children, livestock (his wealth), servants, and was left in bad health with a nagging, awful wife. Job said, *"Though He slay me, yet will I trust Him."*

I just wonder if God put money on you today, would He lose it? Would He lose the challenge with the devil if He said, "I've got some people that even if they've got a raggedy car they'll praise Me anyhow. Even if they had to get to church on a bus and had to take the bus to work every day, they'll still praise Me. If they had to be on government assistance, they'll still praise Me."

Praise Brings Light

When you really get into the praises of God, you'll understand that praise is a way of life for the believer. Praise is an attitude of the heart. An attitude is an external sign of an internal feeling. Praise springs out of a heart of gratitude. When you focus your thoughts on who God is in your life, you will find that praise is the response that effervesces from you. You count your blessings and realize all the wonderful things that God has done. Even when things were bad, they could've been worse, but God was faithful to you. You count your blessings.

God inhabits the praises of His people. (See Psalm 22:3.) He makes praise His dwelling place. So if you ever want God to tabernacle with you, house praise in your heart that is generously extended back to God, and God will always be with you. He's just a praise away. He inhabits the praises of His people—not the gripes, criticisms, complaints. There are people that need God desperately, and they're the very ones complaining about it. The way to summon His presence is to praise Him.

Have you ever been in the world with a turmoil in your soul? Start with praise. Praise ushers in the presence of God. God's presence brings His peace. Out of the peace, when everything is at rest in your soul, God will reveal His purpose. When you get God's purpose then God sends power for His purpose. When you get power into your life, power produces provision. But it all begins with the praise. Praise brings the presence; the presence produces His protection; the protection brings His peace; the peace unveils His purpose; the purpose summons the power; and the power produces the provision—in that order. Most people want the provisions, and they never back up to how it all begins with praise. But praise is where you must begin.

If you're experiencing a dark night, you've got the power to turn on the lights supernaturally with your praise. Psalm 57:7–8 says, "*My heart is steadfast, O God. My heart is steadfast. I will sing and give praise. Awake my glory. Awake lute and harp. I will awaken the dawn with my praise.*" I will make the morning come with my praise. You don't have to wait for the sun to get up. The sun will turn on when you open your mouth and begin to praise God. If you're in a dark place, you can start changing your trajectory just by praising God.

When you're in a dark place in your life, if you'll just forget about yourself and exalt and magnify the glorious nature of who God is, I declare to you that you can come out of your darkness. You can turn the light on and cause morning to come in the middle of the night for you. Paul and Silas did this very thing in Acts 16, when they were in the prison. The Bible says, "*At midnight...*" (verse 25). It was dark, but Paul and Silas awakened the dawn! When they were there, their souls were confined into a little room and their hands and feet were in stocks, but at midnight they began to pray and to sing praises and hymns unto God. When they began to sing their praises unto God, somehow the earth shook, and the foundations of the prison were shaken. Everyone's bands were loosed, and the doors fell open.

You can get liberated, delivered from your shackles and chains when you learn to praise God. Paul and Silas didn't praise Him *after* the bands fell off and *after* the doors opened. They praised Him while they were still locked up in the prison. They were still on lockdown, and they praised Him. They were still in the stocks, and they praised Him. They were still under their authority, and they praised Him. You can't wait until you get free to praise Him. Praise Him while you're still bound! That's the way to get free! It was midnight but light came into that place, and everybody's bands were loosed. You know what I really believe? The Bible talks about how the earth is His footstool, and I believe that when Paul and Silas were singing His praise that there was a beat to their music. I believe God, sitting on the throne, happened to tap the footstool of the earth. I believe He tapped the earth that was His footstool, and when He tapped to the beat of their song, the whole place shook, and He shook it until every prison door was opened and until every man's bands were loosed. He dramatically changed the trajectory of Paul and Silas right there in that prison!

You use praise to bring the glory of God into the darkness of your life and of your night, and let the light of God's praise shine in unto you. This is your destiny. Peter writes to believers, "*You are a chosen generation, a royal priesthood, a holy nation, His own special people, that you may proclaim the praises of Him who called you out of darkness into His marvelous light*" (1 Peter 2:9). God's presence will come to you when you need it, for everything you need is in His presence. So when you're in the midst of a difficult transition, praise Him!

18

God's Word of Power
for Your Life

A s we draw near to this book's end, I want to turn your attention to a very interesting story in 1 Kings 13. I'll give you some closing thoughts on this topic of changing your trajectory, so that you can be proactive in preparing yourself to deal with all the vicissitudes of life that this world is sending your way.

This isn't any deep exegesis and hermeneutics. These are just certain thoughts from this passage that have leaped out to me, things that speak to me in a very practical way, showing me again the Lord's revelatory gift and the power of His Word. Remember, when you read the Bible, don't read it as a history book. This is a book overflowing with life lessons. You have to stop and ask, "Lord, what in the world are You saying to me in 1 Kings 13? How does this pertain to my life today?"

The Bible is so God-breathed! It has the life of God in it; there is power in the Word of God. Nothing else can cleanse your mind and purge your consciousness like God's Word can. It's like a surgeon's scalpel; it has the ability to cut out things that have been irritating you and aggravating you. This Word is good for correction, for reproof, for doctrine, for rebuke. It's so meaningful to us. So as I approach the Word of the Lord, I speak to God and say, "Lord, show me what it is that You're saying to me in this moment. What is there in Your Word for me *right now?*"

Prophesy to Your Situation or Condition

This passage we'll study concerns a prophet, "a man of God," whose name we don't know. In those days, King Jeroboam of Israel had sinned by setting up an altar in the city of Bethel, along with an idol of a golden calf. As 1 Kings 13 begins, this king was standing by this altar in Bethel offering incense. Then the prophet, the man of God, "*went from Judah to Bethel **by the word of the Lord**"* (verse 1); he had a message from God for this king in that very place.

And there at the altar in Bethel, the man of God "*cried out against the altar **by the word of the Lord**, and said, 'O altar, altar! Thus says the Lord…'*" (verse 2). He then foretold a coming day when a descendant of David would desecrate this wicked altar by burning human bones upon it (something that would be fulfilled centuries later, as we see in 2 Kings 23:15–16).

This man of God also prophesied a confirming sign: "*Surely the altar shall split apart, and the ashes on it shall be poured out*" (verse 3). God had given him the vision of the altar cracking and spilling out its ashes.

Now take notice especially here of how this man of God cried out against the *altar* by the Word of the Lord. He began his message by saying, "**O altar, altar!** *Thus says the Lord…*." It's interesting that the prophetic word of the Lord in this moment was to an altar; He spoke to a thing, not a person. It's like in Ezekiel 37, where God told Ezekiel to prophesy to dry bones and to the wind.

Here's the message I want you to get here: *Sometimes you need to prophesy to your condition or your situation.* Sometimes it has nothing to do with a person. You need to prophesy to the condition or situation currently at hand. Every now and then, when you've been so vexed by something that's trying to take hold of your mind or body or the life of your child or of someone you love—you need to prophesy to that thing.

The Bible says this about prophecy: *"He who prophesies speaks edification and exhortation and comfort to men"* (1 Corinthians 14:3). In that same passage we're instructed to *"desire spiritual gifts, but **especially** that you may prophesy"* (verse 1), and we're told, *"Desire earnestly to prophesy"* (verse 39). This divinely inspired utterance speaks to people to edify them, to lift them up. But for their sakes and for our own, we also need to be able to prophesy to things and conditions in our life. I don't think that God would have told us to desire earnestly to prophesy if there was no power in it, no power in your own mouth!

Sometimes you ought to get a righteous indignation rising up in your life, and by the authority of Jesus Christ you begin to prophesy to afflictions from the enemy and say, "Enough, Satan! The Lord rebuke you! I've had enough of your interrupting my day and making me dysfunctional! Enough of that! I prophesy to you in Jesus' name that you will stop and desist, that your assignment against this life is annulled in the name of the Lord!" You begin to speak by divine inspiration words that will edify you, words that will strengthen you and comfort you.

When the enemy has brought confusion into your home, stop when you walk through your door, and remember that you're the prophet and the priest of that house. Step in there and take authority and start speaking the Word of the Lord! When sadness and depression and confusion have assaulted your mind or your loved one's mind, draw a line in the sand and begin to prophesy to this thing: "You've attacked us long enough; I bind you, in Jesus' name!"

Just release the prophetic word of the Lord, because His Word will accomplish what God intends. We are His instruments in the earth. He has no other mouth but our mouth. That's why we read, *"Surely the Lord GOD does nothing, unless He reveals His secret to His servants the prophets"* (Amos 3:7). And since we're to earnestly desire to prophesy, there ought to be an earnest expectation in you when you say "Spirit of the living God, fill me with Your words. Fill me with Your power, and let me speak to this condition." When God speaks, living things will lay down and die, and dead things will rise up and live.

You would be surprised how you can change things with the prophetic word of the Lord. So allow Him to do that.

The Prophecy Confirmed

Notice now what happened in response to the man of God's prophecy toward the altar.

First we see something happen to the king:

So it came to pass when King Jeroboam heard the saying of the man of God, who cried out against the altar in Bethel, that he stretched out his hand from the altar, saying, "Arrest him!" Then his hand, which he stretched out toward him, withered, so that he could not pull it back to himself. (1 Kings 13:4)

Whenever you try to arrest what God has ordained, something will wither in you. Let me say it this way: if you attempt to hinder the works of God's hand, He'll hinder the works of your hand.

Then we see something happen to the altar: "*The altar also was split apart, and the ashes poured out from the altar, according to the sign which the man of God had given by the word of the LORD*" (verse 5).

This simply says to us that God confirms His Word. God always confirms His Word by some kind of sign. God always confirms in the earth what He has already declared from the heavens.

It's like the promise God made to Abraham concerning the multitude of his descendants: they would be like the stars in the sky (the promise confirmed in heaven) as well as like the sand on the seashore (the promise confirmed on earth). If you don't have confirmation for something God has said to you, dismiss it. God will always confirm His Word. He has said, "*By the mouth of two or three witnesses the matter shall be established*" (Deuteronomy 19:15). If you get it only once from one source, then it has not yet been confirmed.

When someone is speaking something from God, there ought to be a quickening in your spirit that bears witness to it. The Spirit within us bears witness that we're the children of God. He's given us His Spirit to bear witness on earth. *"And there are three that bear witness on earth: the Spirit, the water, and the blood; and these three agree as one"* (1 John 5:8). God has a way of causing a power of agreement to come where one confirms the other.

IF YOU ATTEMPT TO HINDER THE WORKS OF GOD'S HAND, HE'LL HINDER THE WORKS OF YOUR HAND.

God will speak some things, and then He'll bring about signs. He'll always send a sign, like the sign of the rainbow to confirm His covenant in Noah's day, and like the sign of circumcision to confirm His covenant in Abraham's day. There's a sign of every covenant; there's also a sign for every word God gives to us.

Always look for the sign of God in confirmation, because God doesn't expect you to move on things that He hasn't yet confirmed with you. Wait for that confirmation. God will often confirm it by someone who doesn't know anything about your situation. He'll confirm it by seasoned saints who are close to Him and who have integrity in their hearts.

He'll confirm what He has spoken to you in His Word. He'll confirm it by His Spirit. He will let you know, "That was Me talking to you. That was *Me*. That was not just your flesh, or just your mind, or just a coincidence."

Mercy from God

Now observe what happens next after the king's hand had withered:

Then the king answered and said to the man of God, "Please en-treat the favor of the LORD your God, and pray for me, that my hand may be restored to me." So the man of God entreated the LORD, and the king's hand was restored to him, and became as before. (1 Kings 13:6)

This shows us that God is a merciful God who gives us new oppor-tunities. Morning by morning, His mercies are made new to us. God is a God of mercy. Thank God for His incredible mercy!

The king was repentant in his heart. And when we are repentant, God will restore us, because He's a God of mercy. He gives you new opportunities. Thank God that He is plenteous in mercy; He never runs out of mercy.

Don't Go Back the Same Way

What happens next in the story is quite surprising. Pay close at-tention to this:

*Then the king said to the man of God, "Come home with me and refresh yourself, and I will give you a reward." But the man of God said to the king, "If you were to give me half your house, I would not go in with you; nor would I eat bread nor drink water in this place. For **so it was commanded me by the word of the LORD**, saying, 'You shall not eat bread, nor drink water, nor return by the same way you came.'" So he went another way and did not return by the way he came to Bethel.* (1 Kings 13:7–10)

God had given this prophet not a *suggestion*, but a *commandment*, and it was clear and specific: he was not to linger in Bethel, not even for a meal; he was to return home, but *not* by the same way he had taken to get there.

It's a shame when you hear truth and turn around and go back the same way you came. It's amazing how you can tell people the truth, give them the truth, and they behold the truth—and yet they walk away as though they've not even heard the truth. They go back the same way, because they're such creatures of habit.

It's to our detriment when we keep living as though things are the same, when circumstances in the world happen to be changing all the time. You know a definition for insanity? It's doing the same thing over and over and expecting a different outcome. We have to realize that what brought us to where we are will not take us to where we want to go. There are things that need to change. Otherwise we'll be obsolete. We'll be totally irrelevant in the current culture.

INSANITY IS DOING THE SAME THING OVER AND OVER AND EXPECTING A DIFFERENT OUTCOME.

Likewise, when you've had an encounter with God, you have no business leaving His presence the same way you entered. We're transformed by the presence of the Lord. As we behold Him in worship, something ought to be transformed in us. We're transformed by His incredible presence and power.

So when you've heard from God, don't let anybody turn you around. When you *know* that you know that you know—don't let anybody talk you out of it. Don't let anybody deceive you. There are folks who just don't want to see you succeed. They don't want to see you prosper. They don't want to see you be blessed. They don't want to see you promoted. They'll say things to you that will throw you off. They'll say, "Are you sure you heard God right?"

When you have an experience with God, it's as though something has been altered in you; He stretches you through the exposure to the greater. It changes us, the lesser, into becoming greater.

Our God is a consuming fire—and when you touch fire, do you remain cold, or do you get heated up? The principles of thermodynamics say that energy flows from the higher source to the lower source. You might at first be cold toward some things, but when you come in contact with God, when you touch fire, you'll know it, and it changes you. You don't leave the same.

What Hurts You Is What You Go Back To

As the story goes on in 1 Kings 13, we come to a stunning conclusion. The prophet meets another prophet, an older man, and suddenly he is confronted with an opposing word, a deceptive word, a word that goes against what God has told him. The older man found the prophet, and said, "Come home with me and eat bread" (verse 15).

At first the prophet keeps hold of his instructions from God:

He said, "I cannot return with you nor go in with you; neither can I eat bread nor drink water with you in this place. For I have been told by the word of the LORD, 'You shall not eat bread nor drink water there, nor return by going the way you came.'"

(verses 16–17)

But this older man deceived him:

He said to him, "I too am a prophet as you are, and an angel spoke to me by the word of the LORD, saying, 'Bring him back with you to your house, that he may eat bread and drink water.'" (He was lying to him.) So he went back with him, and ate bread in his house, and drank water.

(verses 18–19)

So the prophet quickly fell for it.

For every gift that God has, the devil has a counterfeit. So when somebody will prophesy, there's another one that will prophe-*lie*. You have to be careful about counterfeits. The prophet should have known that this man was lying. You know somebody's lying when two men claiming to be prophets have messages that are so opposite. They can't both be getting their directions from God.

After the prophet was comfortably eating and drinking in this older man's house, the truth comes out, through the very words of the older man:

And he cried out to the man of God who came from Judah, saying, "Thus says the LORD: 'Because you have disobeyed the word of the LORD, and have not kept the commandment which the LORD your God commanded you, but you came back, ate bread, and drank water in the place of which the LORD said to you, "Eat no bread and drink no water," your corpse shall not come to the tomb of your fathers.'" (1 Kings 13:21–22)

And right away, after the prophet finished his meal, judgment from God fell upon him: *"When he was gone, a lion met him on the road and killed him. And his corpse was thrown on the road, and the donkey stood by it. The lion also stood by the corpse"* (verse 24).

Now here's the message to take from that: *It is not what you go to that hurts you, but what you go back to.* What is it that God has called you away from that you're trying to go back to? Like a dog returning to its own vomit, what is it that you're trying to return to? It's not what you go to that messes you up; you get messed up when you go back to what God has already delivered you from.

It just absolutely blows my mind when I see people in the church who one moment are in love with God in His goodness, and the next moment have fallen out of relationship with Him. They can leave God, who is so good, but they won't leave their bad relationships and bad environments and bad habits! The psychology of that baffles my mind.

Whenever you become frustrated, whenever you come under pressure, whenever you come under stress, there's something in the devil's arsenal that starts putting flesh hooks in you, yanking you back to the last thing that brought you worldly comfort, the last situation or place or person where you found worldly acceptance and appreciation. Yet you know the dangers and issues back there. That's why you left that place to begin with! But it's the trick of the enemy to always try to send you back the same way you came.

God wants us to be transformed by His glory, transformed by His presence; He wants us to be brand new people, transformed by beholding Him. He's called us to a brand new transformation. So this is what we do in Him: we allow ourselves to be transformed by the glory of God.

You must always sow toward your future. And you must always give up something in order to rise higher. You must give up your past in order to possess your future. It's just a principle of life.

Sow and Reap

I love something that C. S. Lewis said: "Nothing that you have not given away will ever really be yours."[11] Until you give joy to others, you'll never truly have joy. Until you give respect to others, you'll never truly have respect. Until you give love, you'll never really experience love. You must first actually give those things away, whatever it is that you really want.

We call that sowing. We reap what we sow. You have to give away whatever it is that you really want in the harvest of your own life.

We have looked in this book at many perspectives and principles that can bring blessing to your life. They can give you wisdom for your journey on the seascape of uncertainty, as God changes your trajectory. I pray that you will sow these things into your life, so that you can begin to experience today a harvest of blessing and righteousness and peace.

You face so many bewildering changes in the world around you. And there will be many more to come. But because of the Lord's mercy and grace, as you trust Him, you have every reason to enjoy His security and fulfillment, His goodness and mercy, all the days of your life—and to dwell in the house of the Lord forever.

May God bless with you joy on this incredible journey!

---

11. C. S. Lewis, *Mere Christianity* (New York: Macmillan, 1952), 190.

About the Author

Dr. Dale C. Bronner has changed his trajectory many times over the course of his life. He started his first job at five years old delivering newspapers. At twelve, he began processing the payroll for his father's business, Bronner Bros. Manufacturing Co., Inc. Over the years, he transitioned through a myriad of jobs in both retail and the ministry. He was called to his first pastorate at age twenty-seven, and founded Word of Faith Family Worship Cathedral two years later, an interdenominational ministry that is now thriving with more than 20,000 members. He is a sought-after conference speaker, a leadership trainer, and the author of *Get A Grip* (1996), *Guard Your Gates* (2002), *A Check Up from the Neck Up* (2003), *Treasure Your Silent Years* (2004), *Home Remedies* (2005), *Pass the Baton* (2006) and *Planning Your Succession* (2008). Bishop Bronner's message reaches millions daily through his international multimedia broadcast. He resides in Atlanta with his wife, Nina. They are the proud parents of four daughters and one son, and the proud grandparents of two beautiful granddaughters and two handsome grandsons.

Welcome to Our House!

We Have a Special Gift for You

It is our privilege and pleasure to share in your love of Christian books. We are committed to bringing you authors and books that feed, challenge, and enrich your faith.

To show our appreciation, we invite you to sign up to receive a specially selected **Reader Appreciation Gift**, with our compliments. Just go to the Web address at the bottom of this page.

God bless you as you seek a deeper walk with Him!

WE HAVE A GIFT FOR YOU. VISIT:

whpub.me/nonfictionthx

WHITAKER
HOUSE